Laying
on of
Stones

D.J. Conway

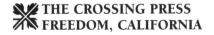
THE CROSSING PRESS
FREEDOM, CALIFORNIA

Library of Congress Cataloging-in-Publication Data

Conway, D. J. (Deanna J.)
    Laying on of stones / by D.J. Conway.
        p. cm.
    Includes bibliographical references and index.
    ISBN 1-58091-029-7 (paper)
    1. Gems—Therapeutic use. 2. Precious stones—Therapeutic use. I. Title.
RM666.P825C66 2000   99-36232
    615.8'9—dc21   CIP

Table of Contents

Illustrations

CHAPTER I

Stones & Their Magical Energies

Humankind has been wearing and using certain stones for healing and magical purposes for thousands of years. Amber, carnelian, and quartz crystal jewelry that dates from the seventh to the fourth millennium B.C.E.[1] has been found in archeological excavations in Mesopotamia. By 400 B.C.E. in India, ancient Sanskrit writings recorded the healing and magical powers of the stones known in that region. The ancient Egyptians left us some of the most complete records of the properties and uses of stones, as well as placing these prized possessions in tombs. Many other cultures around the world, many of which were isolated, assigned identical or similar powers to these stones. Even in this modern era of disbelief in many things, there are still hundreds of thousands of people around the world who wear or use certain stones and strongly believe in their powers to heal, protect, prosper, or bring love. For those readers interested in the history of stones, please consult the Bibliography at the end of this book.

---

1. B.C.E. means Before Common Era and is a non-religious method of marking time. C.E. means Common Era.

All stones have a certain, unique energy, which can be felt or intuited, with a little practice. This energy is electromagnetic in nature and, with the proper scientific equipment, can be physically measured. Most people will choose a stone by holding it in their power hand (the hand used most often in daily life) to decide if that particular stone is for them. When you hold a stone, it may feel hot, cold, vibrating, sharp, or slimy; you may even see pictures or colors in your mind. With a little practice you learn to determine if you can work comfortably with a particular stone or whether you should try another one. If you do not feel comfortable with a stone, don't buy it, no matter how attractive it is or how reasonable the price. The stone's energy simply doesn't match your vibrational energy pattern and may well draw to it—and to you—vibrations you don't want. The size of a stone has no bearing about its importance in magic and healing; bigger does not always mean better. It also does not matter if the stone is natural, tumbled, or faceted, although there is disagreement on this point.

If you purchase stones, buy them from a local rock shop or a reputable seller. The prices in these establishments are usually lower than the prices in many New Age shops. Check the Sources list at the end of this book for addresses and web sites of reputable mail order businesses that sell stones.

Any stone you purchase or find should be cleaned of dust, dirt, and previous vibrations before using it for healing or magic. Stones should also be cleaned after every healing session so that they do not become saturated with the vibrations of disease. All of the stones listed in this book, except turquoise, can be safely cleaned by holding under cool, running water, then drying with a soft towel or cloth. Do not use cold water on opals or turquoise, as the sudden temperature change may shatter the stone. If a stone is dirty in the physical sense, use an old toothbrush to gently remove bits of debris.

To clean a stone by the salt method, bury it in a small bowl of salt, from a period of one hour to two days, depending upon how the stone feels when you take it out of the salt, then rinse thoroughly under cool water and dry. Dispose of the salt, as it is now contaminated with the debris and negative vibrations from the stones. An alternative salt method is to dissolve half a cup of salt in a quart of cool water, soak the stone for several hours, then rinse and dry it.

Quartz crystals can withstand being buried in salt or washed in salt water or cool running water without damage. However, salt or salt water will harm some stones, such as malachite, opal, pearls, and turquoise. Stones mounted in any metal other than 14 K gold or stainless steel also should not be cleaned by the salt method as salt may pit or mar the metal. When in doubt, the safest way is to place it on top of a clear quartz or amethyst cluster. Afterward, hold the stone in the smoke of frankincense or myrrh. This also will cleanse away any negative vibrations.

A few stones will be so contaminated with the vibrations of people who have handled it that it will need to be cleansed by salt or water, then incense smoke, and finally set on a crystal cluster for as long as a month.

You will probably find that you are drawn to collect more than one piece of the same kind of stone. Healing often requires several stones of the same kind. By spending time getting acquainted with each of your stones, you will learn that no two pieces of the same type, for example, will have the same intensity of energy. Each stone is unique and very individual.

All stones that you plan to use for healing and/or magical purposes should be carefully stored away in small, soft bags, boxes, or in a drawer with dividers. Since it is very easy to confuse some of the stones, it is a good idea to label the container. You also want to protect these stone tools from curious people who might indiscriminately handle them, thus either draining their energy or leaving behind unwanted vibrations.

In both healing and in magic, you need to be responsible for the use of your stone energies. You should never heal a person who truly doesn't want to be healed. There are some people who use illness as a way to control family and friends and, deep down, don't want a healing. Never heal a person unless she/he asks to be healed. In magic, you have no right whatsoever to control another person. That brings a karmic reaction you will not want.

Keep an open mind when learning to use the energies of stones. You will not accomplish anything by holding tight to narrow-minded, preconceived ideas. You also will not recognize the unexpected wonders that come your way.

CHAPTER II

Using Stones in the Home & Office

One of the easiest ways to become familiar and comfortable with crystals and stones is to use them in your everyday and/or work environment. Stones or pieces of quartz crystal set in a room seldom draw negative comments any more, but are more likely to elicit curiosity and attract appreciative attention. This means you will have to wash the stones more often than usual to remove the vibrations of the people who simply cannot resist picking them up. Do not let people's handling of the stones bother you. Crystals and stones set about a room act as filters in the environment, straining out negativity and discord. The whole idea of using stones as part of your decoration in a home or office is to create a more peaceful, inspiring atmosphere in which to live and work.

Please note that it is unwise to hang or place quartz crystals where hot sunlight, particularly afternoon sunlight, can shine through them. Crystals act as magnifiers and can start fires in cars and homes in this way. Also, sunlight is detrimental to the energy of quartz crystals, unlike many other more opaque stones; moonlight, however, will enhance the power.

Every home and office has what I call "dead" areas: sections of a room where energy gathers and stagnates or seems to be devoid of positive energy. This can usually be felt in corners, but can be detected in other areas as well. The placement of stones in these dead areas, or at least somewhere within the main traffic area of the room, will help to reverse this condition.

Rooms often seem totally devoid of energy, making them unpleasant to be in and potentially attractive to negative vibrations. This can occur in rooms where the door faces a window directly. This straight-through flow allows the energy to speed through the room, leaving only emptiness behind. If possible, hang a crystal from the ceiling, in direct line between the door and window. This will slow the passage of energy and force it to curve to both sides, sweeping both sides of the room and clearing out stagnant pockets.

Working in an office where stiff competition abounds and hard decisions are made daily can be a draining experience. If you have a separate office or cubicle for yourself, you can build a temporary shelter from the storm of negative energy flying about such businesses. On your desk, place a selection of stones or crystals between you and the door. This will deflect the randomly swirling negative energy and allow you to work with greater mental ease.

A stress-bowl can also aid in relieving stress, thus its name. Fill an attractive bowl with small pieces of crystal or other helpful stones. When you need to relax, run your fingers through the stones; this will help to draw out the stress and tension. You may well find that those who enter your office space soon will be doing the same thing even though they might not understand why. If you use a stress-bowl at home, provide it with a cover. Children and pets can have the stones spread throughout the house in a short time. It can be quite shocking to unexpectedly step on a stone with your bare foot, when half-asleep in the morning.

If possible, place a sizable piece of an appropriate stone on a table in a corner of a room or any area where you feel uncomfortable. This will either deflect the negative energies pooling there or change them into positive vibrations. If you have a file cabinet in the corner, use it as a stand for your stone.

Sometimes it becomes necessary to use a combination of stones to cleanse and rebuild the positive energies in an office or room. Place a piece of clear quartz crystal, black onyx, and pyrite in a triangular pattern on a desk or table. This will cleanse, protect, and draw both positive energies and inspiration. If you have a meditation area, use clear quartz crystal and amethyst to raise the vibrations to a more spiritual level. If you or your children have a regular study area, place within it a piece of chrysocolla, black obsidian or onyx, and a quartz crystal. This will help focus the mind, recall needed information, and take away some of the tension.

Small crystals and stones are also helpful if you are having difficulty with a houseplant. Put the stone or crystal in the pot with the plant. Quartz crystal, especially, will charge the soil with healing energy. When the plant recovers, clean the stone and use it for other purposes. I do not believe in wasting nature's gifts by permanently and indiscriminately burying them or throwing them away. Even broken stones or crystals have a place in the stress-bowl. The supply of stones is finite. We should not be wasting them. However, placing or burying quartz crystals at the foundation corners of a house or business building is certainly wise and appropriate, as they will be working for a long time.

Placing a list of goals you want to achieve under a crystal is a sure-fire way to speed up their manifestation. To further empower this list and crystal, place them under a pyramid, even if it is one made out of cardboard. Align one side of the pyramid to true north and put it in a place where it will not be accidentally disturbed. Periodically, cross off the goals as they are reached or make up a new list.

Study the powers of stones and then let your instincts lead you to using them in your home or business. There are no limits to the ways stones can improve your life and environment.

CHAPTER III

The Chakras & Auras

A working knowledge of the chakras or light centers and auras is an important part of stone healing. In ancient times humankind in various civilizations and centers around the world was much more knowledgeable about the "total human" than we are today. Ancient teachings describe a number of distinct, yet interpenetrating, bodies that make up each individual.

Each body has a different rate of vibration and makes a different contribution to the development of the whole human. The most important of these bodies are the physical, etheric or aural, and the soul or spirit. The physical body is the most familiar to us because its vibrations are very dense and make the body visible. The second body is the etheric, which has a higher vibrational rate and is commonly seen as the aura. The chakras exist within this aural body and are connected to the physical body by way of the ductless glands and the nervous system. The soul or spiritual body has the highest vibrations, contains the essence of the real you that is carried from lifetime to lifetime, and is a direct connection with the Supreme Deity.

According to ancient Sanskrit teaching there are seven major light centers in the aura, or etheric body (Fig. 1), that surrounds the physical body and appear to radiate out from the spinal region. The Hindus call these centers "chakras," which means literally "wheels of fire." When seen with the psychic sight, these centers do resemble spinning wheels of brilliantly colored light, each with a different color center. All chakra colors are pure, not dark or muddy. Muddied or impure colors signal a blockage or the presence of a possible disease or potential problem.

The size, shape, and intensity of the colors of the chakras reveal the development and health of each individual. It is not uncommon for one or more chakras to be partially blocked or underdeveloped. This indicates areas in the physical, mental, emotional, or spiritual attitudes that need to be carefully contemplated and corrected or the first stages or actual presence of physical disease or imbalance.

A word of caution here: Do not under any circumstances try to awaken only certain light centers. This applies especially to a deliberate attempt to raise the kundalini, also known as the "serpent fire" or "sacred cobra." The kundalini lies coiled deep within the root chakra and will rise of its own accord when a person is spiritually prepared for it. Premature, deliberate raising of this serpent fire without the spiritual growth and enlightenment to control it is very dangerous. The initial rush may be exhilarating, but there is eventually a short circuit or burnout, beginning in the etheric body and spreading rapidly into the mental, emotional, and physical states as well. The result can be anything from deadly diseases to serious mental imbalance.

Root Chakra

The first chakra, called the root chakra, is located at the base of the spine (Fig. 1A). Its color is red and the associated glands are the ovaries or testes. It corresponds to physical needs, the reproductive organs, procreative powers, and physical survival. Its degree of development sets the pattern for success or failure, the establishment of goals, and the will power to search for enlightenment. Clearing this center is used to treat circulation, depression, infertility, bringing on the menses, anemia, frostbite, neuralgia, and paralysis.

Spleen Chakra

The spleen chakra, called the belly chakra by some, is midway between the root chakra and the navel (Fig. 1B). Its color is orange and the associated glands are the adrenals. It transforms lower vibrational energy into the higher types of energy. This chakra controls the mental attitudes and directly affects the physical and mental. Since it has been established that a high percentage of all disease is brought about by mental or emotional thoughts or traumas, partial or total blockage of this chakra is common. Problems in this light center will be exhibited in varying degrees of nervousness, eczema and other "hard-to-cure" skin rashes, intestinal ulcers, kidney infections and stones, constipation, coughs, exhaustion, menstrual cramps, arthritis, mood elevation, sexual disorders, the kidneys, and lower back trouble.

Solar Plexus Chakra

The solar plexus chakra is located near the navel (Fig. 1C) and traditionally is said to contain vast bundles of vital nerves that join other nerve bundles near the heart chakra. Its color is yellow, and the associated glands are the islands of Langerhans located on the pancreas. It is sometimes referred to as the second brain or lower mind. Blockage in this light center is

The Major Chakras

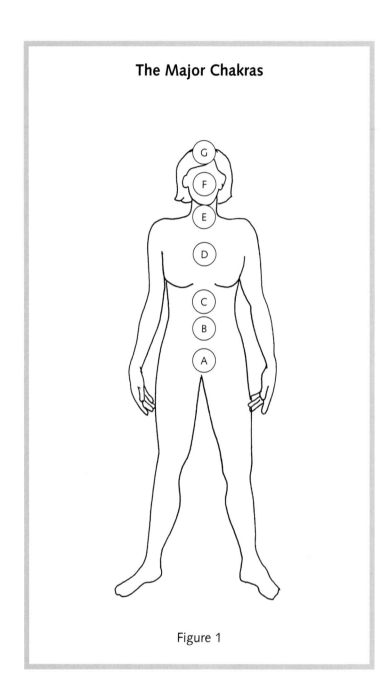

Figure 1

associated with stomach ulcers, diabetes, insomnia, colds, flu, empathy, dispelling fear, exhaustion, digestion, constipation, psychic development, learning, and self-knowledge.

Heart Chakra

The heart chakra is located in the center of the upper chest and a little behind the physical heart (Fig. 1D). Its color is green and the associated gland is the thymus. This light center deals with the higher emotions, compassion, spiritual love, self-respect, and incentive. Treat this light center for diseases of the heart and lungs, stomach and intestinal trouble, ulcers, the eyes, sunburn, love loss or loneliness, headaches, infections, and difficulty with the blood and the bones.

Throat Chakra

The throat chakra is in the front area of the throat just above the collarbone (Fig. 1E). Its color is light electric blue, and the associated gland is the thyroid. When fully developed, this center creates devotional and mystical ideas as well as strengthening clairaudience, or hearing on the etheric level. Use healing on this chakra for pain, burns, sleep, calming, headaches, inflammations, infections, swelling, fevers, menstrual cramps, laryngitis, colds, flu, tonsillitis, mastoiditis, and irritations of the throat, the sinuses, and the nose.

Brow Chakra

The brow chakra is located in the center of the forehead, between and a little above the eyes in the area of the psychic third eye (Fig. 1F). Its color is indigo (bluish purple), and the associated gland is the pineal. Positive traits developed here are clairvoyance, healing, spiritual intuition, and etheric color perception. Work healing on this center to help with headaches, muscle spasms in the neck and shoulders, problems in the legs, knees, and feet, deafness, mental and nervous troubles, negativity, mind clearing, inspiration, pneumonia, and nose and eye diseases.

Crown Chakra

The crown chakra is on top of the head (Fig. 1G). Its color is violet to white to the rarely seen gold, and the associated gland is the pituitary. This light center is the area of supreme spiritual awakening. Treat this light center for sleep inducement, stress, stress diseases, nervousness, cataracts, calming, mental disorders, the scalp and the skull, and tumors.

Transpersonal Chakra

The transpersonal chakra, which in many systems is considered to be the eighth chakra, is located several inches above the head and is not directly connected with the body at all. This light center, which expresses oneness with all things, is associated with white or a rainbow effect, such as is seen in clear quartz crystal, its stone. Physical diseases are not connected with this chakra; rather, it is associated with clearing, building a rapport with the universe and all humankind, vitalizing, protection, and unification.

Minor Chakras

There are also a number of minor chakras: in the palm of each hand, in the sole of each foot, behind each eye, in front of each ear where the jawbone connects, above each breast, at the back of each knee, and on the tips of the fingers. Other than the eight major chakras listed above, you will only be using the foot chakras, which ground, draw energy from the Earth, and return it, and the highly sensitive palm chakras, which can send energy (such as in laying on of hands) and help with the flow of energy from the crown chakra back to the root chakra.

When you use the correct corresponding stone on each chakra during a healing, the combination of stones acts as a catalyst for change. As receptors and transmitters of astral and spiritual light, the stones force the energy to flow naturally from the root chakra up through the crown chakra.

Sometimes a healer will choose to use all of one type of stone on the chakras. This should be done with great caution and an understanding of whether the patient will be able to handle such a strong current of energy.

All clear quartz crystal on the chakras results in a powerful overall balancing and harmonizing. They will cleanse the aura and unblock the chakras. They will also absorb negativity from the aura. People with nervous conditions or who suffer from depression may not be able to tolerate only quartz crystals on their chakras. They may respond better to all green stones, which results in an overall nourishing and balancing effect.

On rare occasions, you can use all black stones on the chakras, but this must be done with extreme care. Black stones can ground and stabilize, but they also can plunge an emotionally unstable person into a deep depression. Black stones are best used on a person who is truly seeking to understand present effects of past lives and is willing to do much truthful soul searching and meditation.

I do not recommend using all red, yellow, or orange stones. These stones, when used on all the chakras, create too much of the purely physical types of energy and will quickly overload the body and aura, causing an extreme nervousness or aberrant behavior.

When healing other people, a healer can determine which chakras are blocked by using a pendulum over each light center. First determine which pendulum movements express yes, no, or maybe. For me, the pendulum swings toward and away from me for a yes, sideways for a no, and in a circle for maybe. This method will help to discover which light centers need in-depth treatment. Follow the pendulum diagnosis with healing through the laying on of stones.

If you do not have time to do a complete chakra healing but need to provide temporary help, you can use a pendulum to determine which chakra is the worst and then have the patient wear a corresponding stone until you have time to do a full healing.

If you are trying to discover which of your own centers are blocked, you will need to use a slightly different method. Cut one-inch squares of correctly colored paper or lens plastic matched correctly to each chakra. Lens plastic is especially good and can be found in photographic stores. Beginning with the red for the root chakra and working up to the violet for the crown, hold the appropriately colored square in the palm of your hand. Hold the pendulum with your power hand over the colored square and ask if that matching chakra needs work. If the chakra is unbalanced or low in energy, the pendulum will swing in a clockwise direction, not stopping until the correction is made. Some chakras will cause the pendulum to swing for some time while others will not cause the pendulum to respond at all. Continue doing this until you have treated all the chakras. However, this is only a temporary measure and should be reinforced with stone healing at the first opportunity.

A word of caution: Never reject standard medical treatment or advise anyone else to do so. This will land you in trouble with the AMA and the law, and it is not a sensible approach to take toward healing. All forms of healing should work together for the good of the patient. Frequently, supplemental stone healing shortens the time needed for standard medical treatment to work, hastening the patient's recovery.

CHAPTER IV

Stone Patterns For Healing

The use of stones in healing is a very ancient practice that is once again coming back into use. As with all types of metaphysical and/or alternative healing, please use this method in conjunction with standard medical treatment. Never advise anyone against seeking or using standard medicine, but use stone healing as an additional method.

All healing with stones laid on the body should last no longer than fifteen minutes at any one session. When first working these stone patterns on a new patient, be aware of the patient's body language of comfort or discomfort while the stones are in place. Some people are unable to tolerate the stones for even five minutes in the beginning. Clear quartz crystal can be added to any of these magical stone patterns, especially above the head and below the feet. Used on some people, clear quartz crystal appears to increase overall power while on others it seems to tone down and smooth out the power of the other stones. It may take two or three healing sessions before some patients can tolerate the quartz crystals at the head, the feet, and the hands.

At no time should you ever tape stones directly to the body

and leave for any length of time! This in itself can cause an imbalance, creating even greater problems.

Have the patient dress in comfortable clothing and lie flat on the back. Do the healing in a calm, quiet place where you will not be interrupted. Playing soft instrumental background music will help the patient to relax. Take your time and do not rush.

Ask the patient to close her/his eyes and concentrate only on the music and the visual image of floating comfortably on a fluffy cloud, a calm lake, or a big bed. You might wish to discuss which you will suggest by talking to the patient before the healing. Some people have a great fear of heights or of water and will not be comfortable if you use these suggestions. Assure them that at no time will they have the sense of falling, but will remain calm and comfortable.

It is quite common for the patient to see colors and/or scenes within the mind while the healing is being performed. These pictures may range from actual past experiences to symbolic visualizations. Encourage the patient to think seriously about these as they will be of significance.

To begin a stone healing, first arrange the stones required gently on the appropriate places on the body, working from the feet or the root chakra up to the crown or transpersonal point. Then position the larger clear quartz crystals, if appropriate, in the outer pattern. If the pattern calls for quartz crystals on the hands, place them on the patient's open palms. Do not be alarmed if the patient clutches these crystals during a healing. This action is an indication of a deep bodily and aural need.

Activate the outer stones or crystals by tapping each one gently in the pattern sequence explained in the description of each stone pattern. These stones or crystals will automatically activate at your touch and energize the other stones situated on the body. After each healing, take care to thoroughly wash all used stones and crystals under cool running water. Stones that cannot be cleansed in water should be set on a crystal cluster, as described earlier.

At the end of each healing, have the patient sit up slowly to avoid nausea, dizziness, or disorientation.

Chakra Stones

There are several stones that are appropriate for each of the chakras. I have listed here only those stones directly mentioned in this book.

Chakra	Stone
1st root	garnet
2nd spleen	carnelian
3rd solar plexus	tiger's-eye
4th heart	green tourmaline, watermelon tourmaline
5th throat	lapis lazuli
6th brow	fluorite
7th crown	amethyst
transpersonal	clear quartz crystal

General Chakra Cleansing

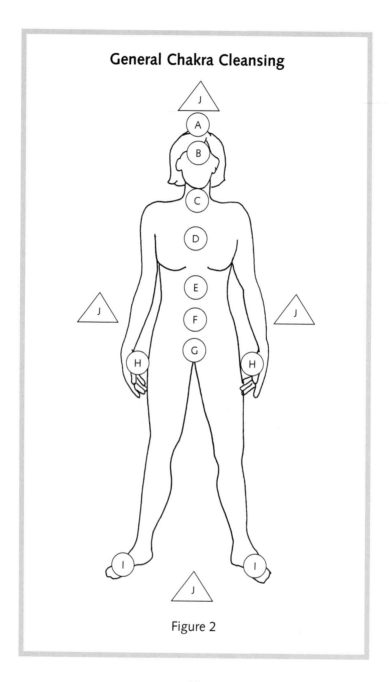

Figure 2

General Chakra Cleansing

Everyone gets her/his seven major chakras out of balance, polluted, or partially closed merely from trying to live in this modern, fast-paced life. This stone pattern (Fig. 2) will gently open, realign, cleanse, and balance the energy flowing through the chakras, not only healing, but also making everyday life a little easier to handle.

Stones needed: four large clear quartz crystals for the outer pattern (Fig. 2J); one small clear quartz point to be set near the crown of the head (Fig.2A); one amethyst for the brow (Fig 2B); one lapis lazuli for the throat (Fig. 2C); one rose quartz for the heart (Fig. 2D); one tiger's-eye for the abdomen (Fig. 2E); one carnelian for the spleen area (Fig. 2F); one garnet for the root (or genital) area (Fig. 2G); one small crystal point for the palm of each hand (Fig. 2H); and brown agate, one to be placed near the sole of each foot (Fig. 2I).

This outer pattern of clear quartz crystals forms a double triangle (diamond shape), or two triangles set base to base. Activate this crystal energy flow by tapping the large crystal at the head, down to the one by the left hand, descend to the crystal at the feet, up to the one by the right hand, and ascend to join the crystal at the head again. This outer pattern will automatically activate the inner pattern of stones on the chakras.

Stress Reliever

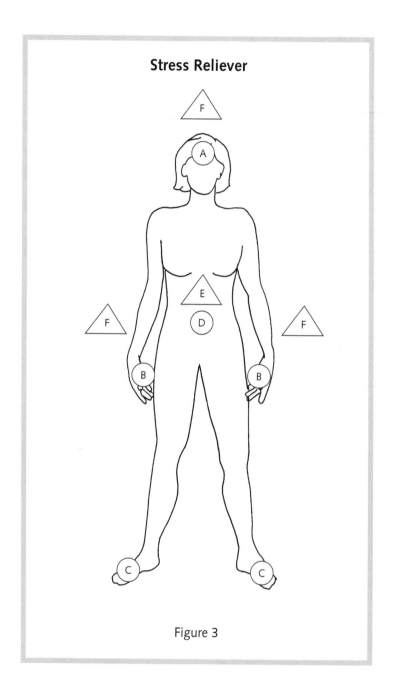

Figure 3

Stress Reliever

A great many diseases are brought about by a weakening of the body and its natural defenses in some manner through stress. To begin healing, stress must be greatly reduced or eliminated. Sometimes stress has become such a part of the life pattern that a boost of some kind is needed to get the patient headed in the right direction. The stone pattern called Stress Reliever is an excellent place to begin, as well as a gentle way to introduce a patient to stone healing.

Stones needed: three large clear quartz crystal points (Fig. 3F); one amethyst for the brow (Fig. 3A); two small amethyst points, one for the palm of each hand (Fig. 3B); two pieces of black onyx, one to be placed near the sole of each foot (Fig. 3C); and one piece of rose quartz and one small clear crystal point (point upward) to be placed on the abdomen near the navel (Fig. 3D, E).

Amethyst on the brow chakra and in the palms of both hands not only stabilizes, grounds, and calms through the minor chakras in the palms, it also encourages the flow of energy to rise to the crown chakra, gush from this light center, and then descend smoothly to rejoin the root chakra. Black onyx absorbs and releases all negatives, thus reducing stress, while rose quartz balances the yin/yang (male/female energies) and rejuvenates. Clear quartz crystal detoxifies the entire aura, the astral bodies, and the chakras. At the same time it will bring harmony and help with clear thinking.

The Stress Reliever sets up two separate triangle areas of energy. The top triangle begins at the crystal above the head, descends to the crystal near the patient's left hand, crosses to the crystal by the right hand, and ascends to join the crystal at the head. Activate the stones in this triangle first by tapping the crystals in this sequence first.

The lower triangle consists of the rose quartz and small crystal on the abdomen, descends to the black onyx by the left foot, crosses to the black onyx at the right foot, and ascends to rejoin the rose quartz. Activate the stones in this triangle last by tapping them in the sequence given.

Colds & Flu

Stones needed: one blue lace agate, one amber, two carnelian, one lapis lazuli, one malachite, two green tourmaline, one turquoise, and two rose quartz.

Blue lace agate works well on hoarseness and sore throat, while the lapis lazuli will aid in clearing out throat congestion. The rose quartz will soothe any sinus pain. Turquoise helps the lungs and the entire respiratory system, as does carnelian. Amber is a wonderful purifier and works well on the ears and general infection. Malachite, a stone of the heart chakra, can purify the blood and balance the entire system. Green tourmaline is for detoxifying the aura and chakras.

The green tourmaline goes on both the root and spleen chakras (Fig. 4B). Put malachite on the heart chakra (Fig. 4C) with a piece of carnelian just above it and to both sides (Fig. 4D). Both blue lace agate and lapis lazuli should go on the throat chakra, just above the collarbone (Fig. 4E, F). Rose quartz goes on each side of the nose over the sinuses (Fig. 4G), while amber rests on the third eye in the center of the forehead (Fig. 4H). Place the turquoise resting against the top of the head (Fig. 4A) so it will open the crown chakra and provide a flow of energy through the body.

Colds and Flu

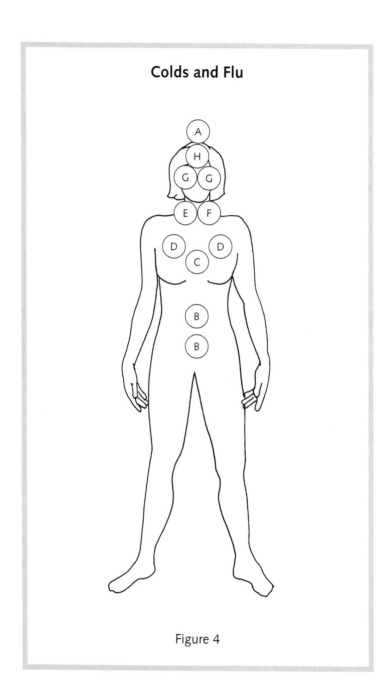

Figure 4

Infertility

Stones needed: one garnet, one rose quartz, two carnelian, and two moss agate.

It is to be hoped that the prospective mother is striving to entice an enlightened soul to come into her life instead of just any soul so she can have a baby. Garnet placed at the root chakra area will stimulate the ovaries and uterus (Fig. 5A). Rose quartz at the heart chakra (Fig. 5B) sets up a vibration to attract a compatible soul that does not have a lot of karmic baggage that might make the family miserable with its appearance. Moss agate, just below and on both sides of the garnet (Fig. 5C), not only stimulates fertility, but also sends out vibrations of universal love. Carnelian, just above and to both sides of the garnet (Fig. 5D), heals and balances the female organs and helps with the reproductive cycle.

In this healing, the rose quartz on the heart chakra should be placed into position first so that the love vibrations, not the lower reproductive ones, will dominate.

Infertility

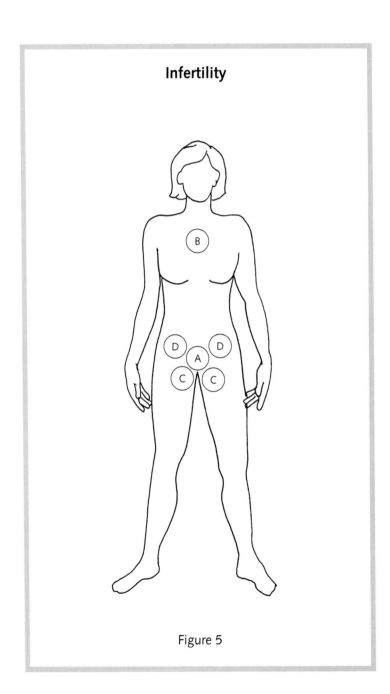

Figure 5

Stomach & Intestinal Disorders

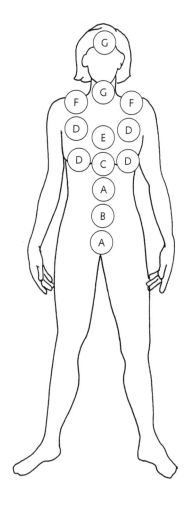

Figure 6

Stomach & Intestinal Disorders

Stones needed: one brown agate, two orange and brown agate, one amber, one carnelian, four tiger's-eye, two amethyst, and two green tourmaline.

Brown agate is a traditional healing stone for indigestion and nausea. The orange and brown agates, placed just below the tip of the breastbone, soothe and heal disease within the stomach itself. Amber, carnelian, and tiger's-eye all work directly on the entire digestive system, toning, balancing, and healing, while green tourmaline works primarily on the intestines themselves. Amethyst not only diminishes pain but cleanses the blood.

Place green tourmaline on both the root and solar plexus chakras (Fig. 6A), with brown agate on the spleen chakra in between (Fig. 6B). Carnelian goes on the heart chakra (Fig. 6C), with a piece of tiger's-eye on each side of it (Fig. 6D). Rest a piece of amber just above the breastbone (Fig. 6E) and a piece of tiger's-eye on each side of the amber (Fig. 6D). Orange and brown agate goes just above the tiger's-eye (Fig. 6F), while amethyst is placed on both the throat and brow chakras (Fig. 6H).

Headaches

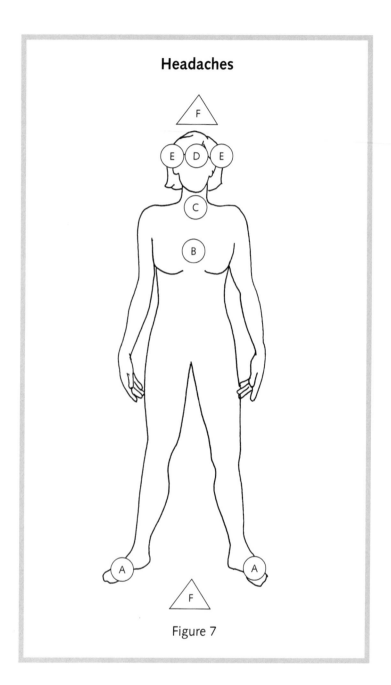

Figure 7

Headaches

Stones needed: one amethyst, one chrysocolla, two hematites, one lapis lazuli, two black obsidians, and two clear quartz crystals.

The black obsidian near the sole of each foot (Fig. 7A) will ground, protect, and absorb any negatives within the patient's aura and chakras. Lapis lazuli on the heart chakra (Fig. 7B) is for calming the patient as well as purifying the aura and light centers, while the chrysocolla at the throat chakra (Fig. 7C) eases headaches and tension and strengthens the connection between the lower and higher light centers. Amethyst on the brow (Fig. 7D) will help soothe the pain. The hematite on each side of the amethyst (Fig. 7E) is another calming stone that lessens stress, a major cause of headaches. The clear crystal quartz below the feet and at the transpersonal point above the head (Fig. 7F) creates a detoxifying flow of energy that will clear blockages from all the chakras, clean the aura, and in general create a state of general well-being in the patient.

Insomnia

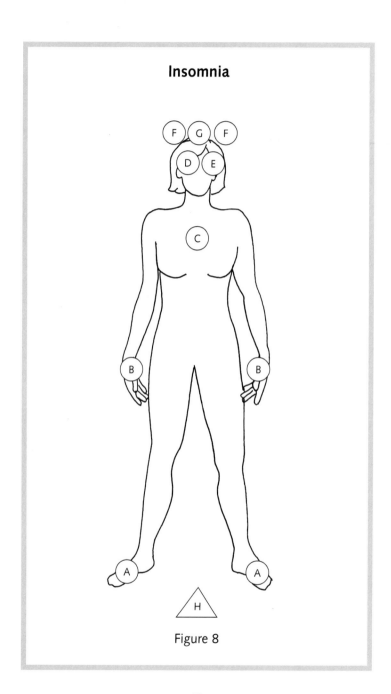

Figure 8

Insomnia

Stones needed: one amethyst, two hematite, two lapis lazuli, one chrysocolla, one green fluorite, one purple fluorite, two black obsidian, and one clear quartz crystal.

To break the cycle of insomnia, the patient must relax and calm the nerves. This can be done through the use of green fluorite and purple fluorite for the nerves and hematite for relaxation. Chrysocolla can balance the emotions, again relieving stress. Amethyst will ease mental problems, create a mild sedated feeling, and break the negative pattern established by not sleeping. Lapis lazuli also works on breaking the insomnia; a powerful all-healing stone, it dispels negative moods and protects from outside influences that may be contributing to the problem. Using black obsidian with clear quartz crystal will not only stabilize and calm, but will detoxify the aura and chakras.

Place a piece of black obsidian near the sole of each foot (Fig. 8A) and a piece of hematite in the palm of each hand (Fig. 8B). Chrysocolla goes on the heart chakra (Fig. 8C), while both green and purple fluorite are placed on the brow chakra (Fig. 8D, E). Two pieces of lapis lazuli (Fig. 8F), with a piece of amethyst between them (Fig. 8G), stimulates the crown chakra. The quartz crystal is placed between the feet and pointed toward the head.

Heart & Circulation Problems

Stones needed: two lapis lazuli, one turquoise, one orange and brown agate, two watermelon tourmaline, one chrysocolla, one chrysoprase, one amber, two amethyst, one purple fluorite, one garnet, two hematite, and two green tourmaline.

All-purpose healing stones for the heart are green tourmaline and watermelon tourmaline. Amber purifies the entire system, while garnet and lapis lazuli specifically cleanse the blood. Use amethyst to prevent or remove blood clots. If you suspect high blood pressure may be involved, use hematite and rose quartz. If stroke has occurred, or may occur from the high blood pressure, purple fluorite and lapis lazuli are good choices to prevent this or help repair previous damage. Other stones used specifically to heal the heart and circulation are turquoise, orange and brown agate, watermelon tourmaline, chrysocolla, and chrysoprase.

Arrange lapis lazuli near the sole of each foot (Fig. 9A) and hematite in the palm of each hand (Fig. 9B). Garnet over the root chakra (Fig. 9C) will propel the energy flow up to the green (Fig. 9D) and watermelon tourmaline (Fig. 9E) placed over the solar plexus. Orange and brown agate on the heart chakra (Fig. 9F) has chrysoprase on the left (your left) (Fig. 9G) of it and chrysocolla on the right (Fig. 9H). Purple fluorite goes on the throat chakra (Fig. 9I). Place amber on the brow chakra (Fig. 9J) between and above the eyes with amethyst on each side (Fig. 9K). Turquoise should be arranged so that it touches the crown chakra (Fig. 9L) at the top of the head.

Heart & Circulation Problems

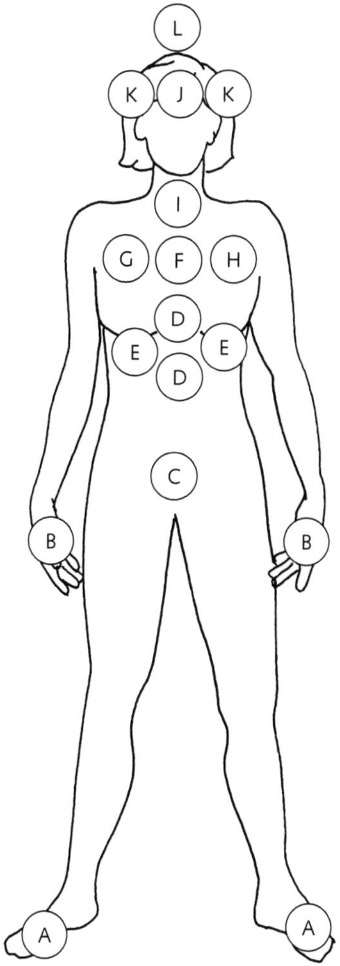

Figure 9

Female Sex Organ Difficulties

Stones needed: two garnet, one carnelian, one orange and brown agate, two chrysocolla, one malachite, one green tourmaline, and one watermelon tourmaline.

Red garnet and carnelian are particularly useful as all-purpose stones in healing female sex organs. Garnet also provides balance in the entire body system and aids in regulating menstruation. Malachite also works well for any menstrual disorders, and has purifying and regenerating powers as well. Cramps can be lessened by placing orange and brown agate and carnelian directly over the uterus. If a hysterectomy is pending, use chrysocolla to balance the uterus and ovaries and prepare that area for surgery. Chrysocolla is also valuable for any type of internal healing. Sometimes problems in the sex organs arise from an imbalance between the lower and upper chakras; to correct this, apply green tourmaline. As a finishing touch, use watermelon tourmaline to correct the yin/yang polarity and induce cell regeneration.

The first stones are placed on the body where the legs join the torso: orange and brown agate on the left (your left) (Fig. 10A) and carnelian on the right (Fig. 10B). Malachite goes over the root chakra (Fig. 10C) with garnet above and to each side of it (Fig. 10D). The patient should have chrysocolla in the palm of each hand (Fig. 10E). Green tourmaline is placed on the heart chakra (Fig. 10F) and watermelon tourmaline on the throat chakra (Fig. 10G).

Female Sex Organ Difficulties

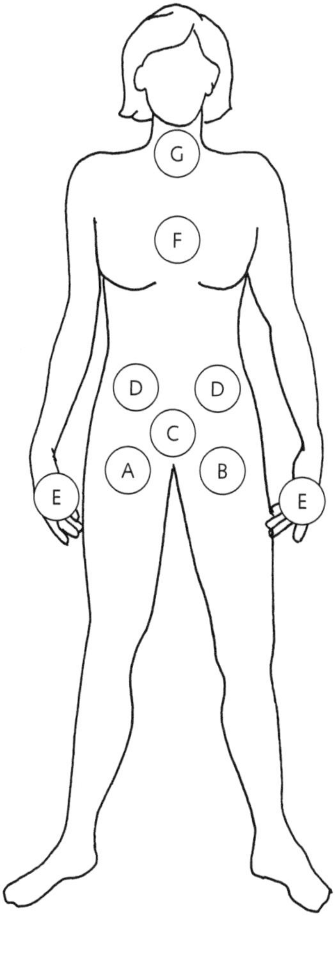

Figure 10

Male Sex Organ Difficulties

Stones needed: two garnet, two chrysocolla, three malachite, one green tourmaline, and one watermelon tourmaline.

Red garnet is an excellent stone to balance the sexual system and to normalize sexuality and the working of the testes. Combined with medical treatment, it can help with prostate problems and impotency. Use chrysocolla for internal healing and malachite to regenerate and purify. Since chakra imbalance can be one of the root causes of problems in the sex organs, use green tourmaline to balance the lower chakras with the upper ones, and watermelon tourmaline to bring the yin/yang polarity back to normal and create cell regeneration.

Arrange chrysocolla near the sole of each foot (Fig. 11A). Two pieces of garnet are arranged over the root chakra (Fig. 11B), while malachite is placed in the palm of each hand (Fig. 11C). Put watermelon tourmaline over the heart chakra (Fig. 11D) and green tourmaline at the throat chakra (Fig. 11E). A piece of malachite is placed touching the top of the head, or the crown chakra (Fig. 11F).

Male Sex Organ Difficulties

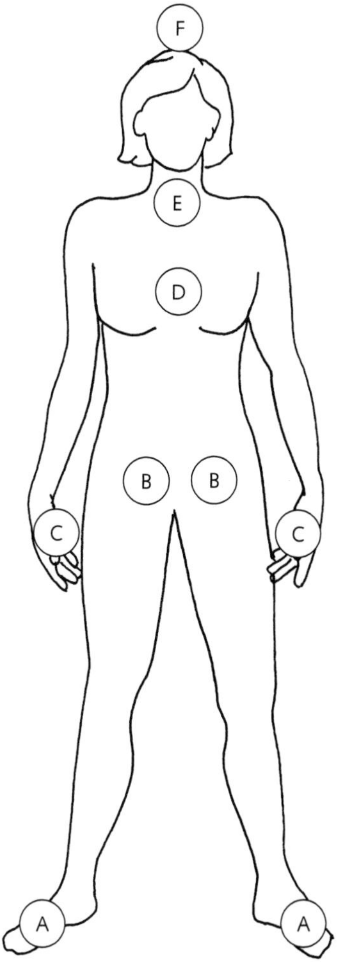

Figure 11

Throat & Thyroid Diseases

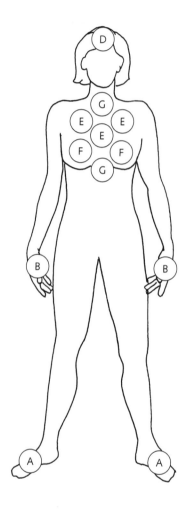

Figure 12

Throat & Thyroid Diseases

Stones needed: three lapis lazuli, two chrysocolla, two blue lace agate, two tiger's-eye, one green tourmaline, two turquoise, and one watermelon tourmaline.

Use lapis lazuli, turquoise, and malachite directly on the throat chakra to help clear out infection and congestion of any kind. Blue lace agate is helpful for hoarseness. Tiger's-eye will purify the blood and respiratory system, while both chrysocolla and lapis lazuli will affect the thyroid gland. To alter negative cell structure and jump-start the healing process, apply green and watermelon tourmaline.

Tiger's-eye is arranged near the sole of each foot (Fig. 12A) and turquoise in the palm of each hand (Fig. 12B). Green tourmaline goes on the spleen chakra (Fig. 12C) and watermelon tourmaline on the brow (Fig. 12D). In the center of the throat chakra put one piece of lapis lazuli and immediately above it, two more pieces (Fig. 12E). Below the centered lapis, place two pieces of chrysocolla (Fig. 12F). Directly below the chrysocolla should be a piece of blue lace agate (Fig. 12G), while immediately above the two pieces of lapis should be another piece of blue lace agate (Fig. 12G).

Healing After Surgery

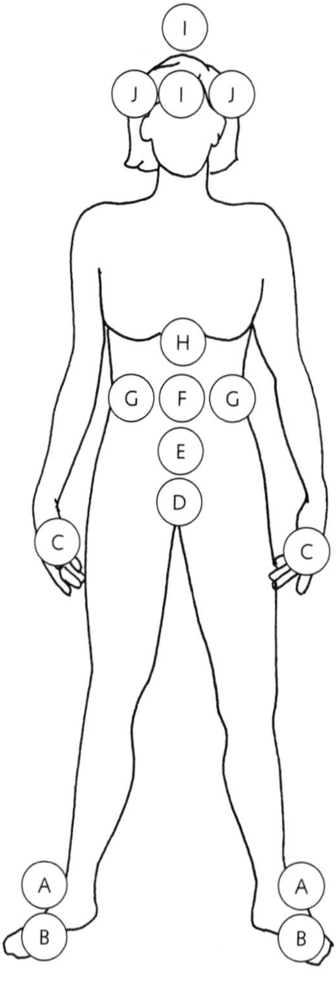

Figure 13

Healing After Surgery

Stones needed: one brown agate, two amber, two amethyst, one chrysocolla, one hematite, two lapis lazuli, three malachite, two black obsidian, two green tourmaline, two watermelon tourmaline, and two bloodstones.

The healer really should not be concerned what the surgery was for, but center her/his attention on healing the physical damage and making the patient as comfortable as possible while the healing is taking place. The accompanying diagram is an example only; place the appropriate stones wherever the incision might be.

Brown agate will ground the patient's energy to the Earth, a powerful energy source in herself, and combat nausea at the same time. To purify, calm, and lessen the damage done by anesthetics, amber is a potent stone. Use amethyst to balance the aura and minimize pain, while chrysocolla will speed internal healing. Lapis lazuli will purify the body and release the pain, and it should be placed directly over the incision. Bloodstone is valuable to stop or prevent any bleeding as well as to renew and revitalize. Combine bloodstone with hematite to control or prevent bleeding. Promote cell regeneration by applying watermelon tourmaline to the incision area, along with malachite, which will heal and balance the entire system. Black obsidian near the soles of the feet will absorb negative energy as well as collect the scattered energy of the patient, making it easier to concentrate upon the healing. Rebalance the lower chakras with the higher ones with green tourmaline; this stone will also detoxify the body and alter negative cell structure.

A piece each of black obsidian (Fig. 13A) and malachite (Fig. 13B) should be arranged near the sole of each foot, while the patient holds green tourmaline in the palm of each hand (Fig. 13C). Watermelon tourmaline goes on the root chakra (Fig. 13D), chrysocolla on the spleen chakra (Fig. 13E), and hematite on the solar plexus (Fig. 13F). On each side of the hematite should be a piece of bloodstone (Fig. 13G). Brown agate goes directly under the lower edge of the breastbone (Fig. 13H). A piece of amethyst should go on both the brow (Fig. 13I) and crown chakras (Fig. 13I), while amber rests on each side of the brow chakra stone (Fig. 13J). Carefully put as many pieces as you wish of lapis lazuli, watermelon tourmaline, and malachite directly on the incision area.

Fevers

Stones needed: one moss agate, one chrysocolla, one lapis lazuli, one rose quartz, two black onyx, and two green tourmaline.

Use green tourmaline and black onyx to balance the chakras and reduce stress. The moss agate, chrysocolla, and lapis lazuli work directly on the fever, helping to lower the temperature of the body and cleanse it. Rose quartz helps to rejuvenate and give a more positive outlook to recovery.

Arrange black onyx near the sole of each foot (Fig. 14A) and green tourmaline in the palm of each hand (Fig. 14B). Rose quartz goes immediately over the heart chakra (Fig. 14C) with chrysocolla just below it (Fig. 14D). Lapis lazuli goes to the right side (your right) (Fig. 14E) and moss agate to the left of the rose quartz (Fig. 14F).

Fevers

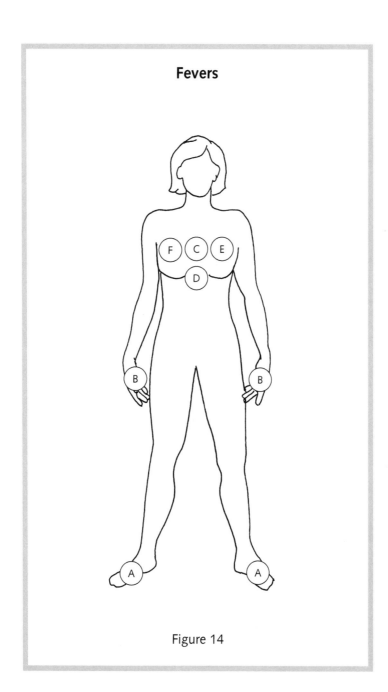

Figure 14

Blood Cleansing

Stones needed: two orange and brown agate, one amethyst, one garnet, two lapis lazuli, two amber, two bloodstone, two hematite, two malachite, and one green tourmaline.

Orange and brown agate, amethyst, red garnet, and lapis lazuli are all very useful in cleansing the blood and circulatory system of any disease, imbalance, or impurities. Malachite and green tourmaline also are specifics for blood cleansing. Use amethyst to prevent or dissolve blood clots, and hematite and bloodstone to prevent or stop unnatural bleeding. Amber is wonderful for purifying the entire physical body system.

Bloodstone (Fig. 15A) should be placed closest to the sole of each foot, with orange and brown agate below it (Fig. 15B). The patient should have amber in the palm of each hand (Fig. 15C). Put garnet on the root chakra (Fig. 15D) and green tourmaline on the spleen (Fig. 15E). Two pieces each of malachite (Fig. 15F) and hematite (Fig. 15G) go on the solar plexus. Lapis lazuli is placed on both the throat (Fig. 15H) and brow chakras (Fig. 15H), while amethyst rests against the crown of the head (Fig. 15I).

Blood Cleansing

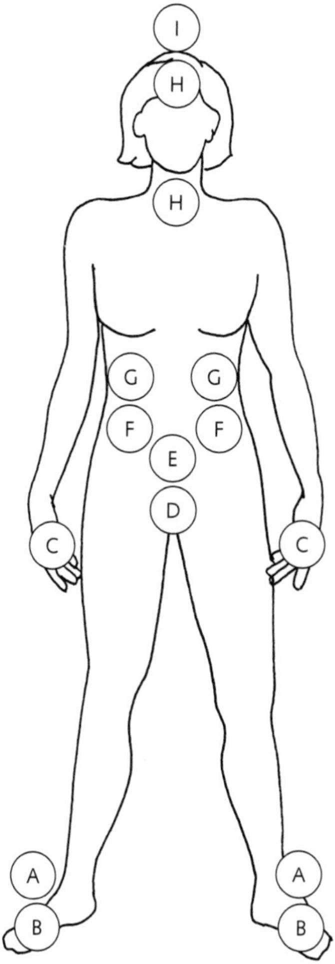

Figure 15

Sinus & Ear Infections

Stones needed: four amber, four rose quartz, two amethyst, and three clear quartz crystals.

Sinus infections are often accompanied by some degree of ear infection or problem. Use amber to purify the entire physical body system. Amber and rose quartz work directly on the ears, while amethyst and rose quartz will impact the sinuses directly.

The stone arrangement for this healing concentrates on the throat and head area. Place amber at both the throat (Fig. 16B) and crown chakras (Fig. 16B). Rose quartz goes just below the nostrils and off a little to each side (Fig. 16C), while amethyst is placed directly above the curved portion of the nostrils on each side of the nose (Fig. 16D). Amber is again used at the outer corners of each eye (Fig. 16B) and additional rose quartz is placed above and in the center of each eyebrow (Fig. 16C). You can use clear quartz crystal both at the soles of the feet (Fig. 16A) and at the transpersonal point above the head (Fig. 16A) to force a detoxifying flow of energy through the body.

Sinus & Ear Infections

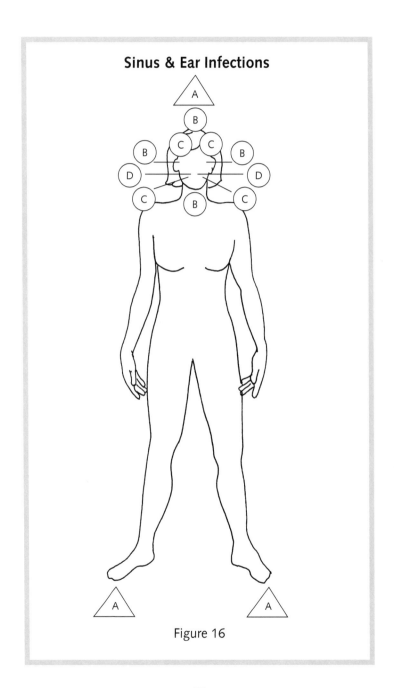

Figure 16

Urinary Tract Infections or Stones

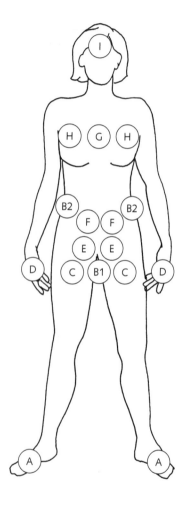

Figure 17

Urinary Tract Infections Or Stones

Stones needed: two orange and brown agates, two bloodstone, two lapis lazuli, one amber, one rose quartz, two malachite, two carnelian, two tiger's-eye, and one or two pieces of garnet.

As anyone who has experienced a urinary tract infection can tell you, this painful disease can manifest in a matter of a few hours with little warning. However painful a UTI is, it is nothing compared to passing, or trying to pass, a kidney stone. Stones as small as the head of a pin can feel like a golf ball; the larger stones require ultrasonic break-up or surgery. Both diseases require immediate medical treatment to avoid long-term damage and to ease the excruciating pain.

Purification is of prime importance in this disease as the system has been clogged with toxins. Use orange and brown agate and red garnet to start the purification process and lapis lazuli and malachite to clean the blood. Amber also cleanses, but it is of more importance in calming and sedating. Bloodstone with its revitalizing strength is particularly useful for bladder problems. Tiger's-eye placed on the solar plexus chakra can repel negative energy that may be coming from outside the patient; it also balances and purifies.

Begin by arranging a piece of tiger's-eye near the sole of each foot (Fig. 17A). Place garnet directly over the bladder (Fig. 17B1) for urinary tract infections or a piece over each kidney (Fig. 17B2) for stones. On each side of the garnet, put malachite (Fig.17C). Carnelian goes in the palm of each hand (Fig. 17D). Two pieces of orange and brown agate are situated over the spleen chakra (Fig. 17E) with two pieces of lapis lazuli directly above them (Fig. 71F). Rose quartz goes over the heart chakra (Fig. 17G) while bloodstone is set to each side of it (Fig. 17H). Amber on the brow chakra (Fig. 17I) will cleanse the upward flowing energy, preparing it for its return through the minor chakras at the soles of the feet.

Coughs & Lung Trouble

Stones needed: two amber, two amethyst, two turquoise, three garnet, two lapis lazuli, two malachite, and two green tourmaline.

Coughs and lung problems always have effects on other parts of the body. Therefore, it is wise to use red garnet to purify the aura and malachite to balance the entire system. Amethyst, amber, turquoise, and chrysocolla work directly on the lungs, while lapis lazuli will work on the infection, wherever it is. Apply green tourmaline to detoxify the respiratory system.

To begin, place green tourmaline near the sole of each foot (Fig. 18A) and malachite in the palm of each hand (Fig. 18B). Amethyst should go on the root chakra (Fig. 18C) and at the crown of the head (Fig. 18C). Garnet is placed on the brow (Fig. 18D), the throat (Fig. 18D), and the heart chakras (Fig. 18D). Pieces of both amber (Fig. 18E) and lapis lazuli (Fig. 18F) are positioned on each side of the garnet over the heart. At the garnet on the throat, put turquoise on each side of that stone (Fig. 18G).

Coughs & Lung Trouble

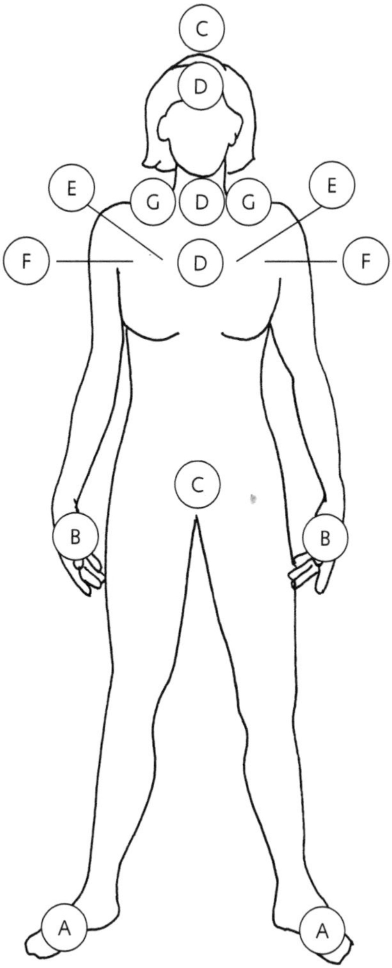

Figure 18

Increasing Physical Energy

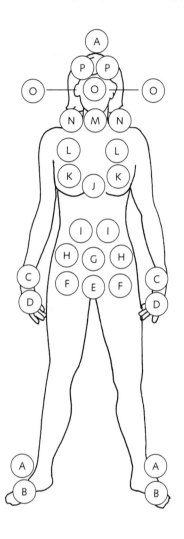

Figure 19

Increasing Physical Energy

Stones needed: three amber, three amethyst, one bloodstone, one carnelian, two chrysoprase, two purple fluorite, two garnet, two hematite, two lapis lazuli, two malachite, two black obsidian, two black onyx, one pyrite, two rose quartz, two tiger's-eye, and one turquoise.

Although a loss of physical energy may arise from stress or disease, it is most often connected with negative thinking or being bombarded by negative thinking. Amber will change any negative energy to positive as well as purify the body, while amethyst centers the concentration and breaks negative patterns. Lapis lazuli and black onyx are valuable in releasing or dispelling negative thoughts or attacks. Use bloodstone to revitalize, carnelian to dispel apathy, and chrysoprase to balance the mental attitudes, all things which must be done to regain energy. Red garnet will attract energy, while hematite and purple fluorite will help the patient to focus that energy to productive uses. If the patient has scattered energy, use black obsidian to aid in collecting it. Rose quartz and pyrite on the heart chakra will promote a more positive outlook on life and aid in uplifting the spirits. To help bring ideas into reality, apply tiger's-eye. For overall balance, turquoise is very useful.

A piece of amber (Fig. 19A) and black obsidian (Fig. 19B) is positioned near the sole of each foot, while a piece of black onyx (Fig. 19C) and chrysoprase (Fig. 19D) is placed in the palm of each hand. At the root chakra put bloodstone (Fig. 19E) with garnet on each side (Fig. 19F). At the spleen chakra center carnelian (Fig. 19G) between pieces of malachite (Fig. 19H). Two pieces of lapis lazuli go on the solar plexus (Fig. 19I). Pyrite goes on the heart chakra (Fig. 19J) between two pieces of rose quartz (Fig. 19K), while two pieces of tiger's-eye are placed just below the collarbone above the heart chakra stones (Fig. 19L). Turquoise (Fig. 19M) is centered between two pieces of purple fluorite on the throat light center (Fig. 19N). On the brow place three pieces of amethyst (Fig. 19O) and over them two pieces of hematite (Fig. 19P). The crown chakra is stimulated by another piece of amber (Fig. 19A), which draws the cleansed energy up from the feet.

The Eyes & Vision

Stones needed: one amethyst, three lapis lazuli, four malachite, two black obsidian, one turquoise, two tiger's-eye, and four green tourmaline.

Stones specifically connected with the eyes and their health are amethyst, lapis lazuli, malachite, black obsidian, and turquoise. Tiger's-eye is also connected with the eyes, particularly with the purification of that area. To regenerate tissue and balance the system, use malachite. Green tourmaline is valuable for detoxifying the aura and chakras.

Green tourmaline (Fig. 20A) and black obsidian (Fig. 20B) should be arranged near the sole of each foot and green tourmaline placed in the palm of each hand (Fig. 20A). Malachite goes on both the root chakra and heart center (Fig. 20C), while lapis lazuli is placed on the throat area (Fig. 20D). On each side of the face, just above the curved portion of the nostrils, place a piece of malachite (Fig. 20C). Place a piece of tiger's-eye (Fig. 20E) and lapis lazuli (Fig. 20F) just above each eyebrow and a piece of turquoise above them and in the center of the forehead (Fig. 20G). Amethyst goes on the crown chakra (Fig. 20H).

The Eyes & Vision

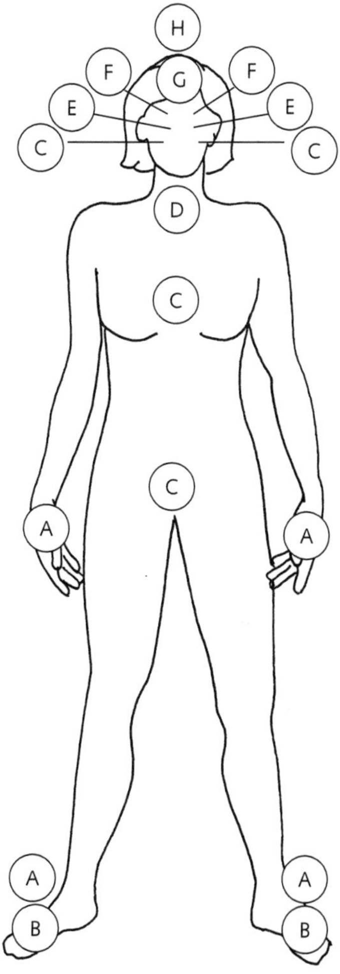

Figure 20

Calming Nervous Energy

Stones needed: two moss agate, two green tourmaline, one amber, one amethyst, two hematite, two orange and brown agate, three malachite, two green fluorite, two purple fluorite, two lapis lazuli, two chrysocolla, one pyrite, and one turquoise.

Excessive nervous energy can be caused by stress-producing situations and people or by mental problems. To begin, the healer must use green tourmaline, moss agate, amber, amethyst, and hematite to sufficiently ground and calm the patient so that healing can take place. Another powerful grounding stone is orange and brown agate. If there are suicidal symptoms or thoughts, amber can help. Amethyst is good for calming the nerves and mental patterns. Green fluorite, malachite, purple fluorite, and lapis lazuli also are helpful in soothing the nerves and mental troubles. Malachite is useful in bringing the entire system back into balance. Use chrysocolla to balance the emotions and hematite to reduce the stress. Pyrite on the heart chakra will rise the spirits and turquoise will give peace.

Position orange and brown agate near the sole of each foot (Fig. 21A) and place malachite in the palm of each hand (Fig. 21B). Pyrite goes on the solar plexus chakra (Fig. 21C) with a piece of hematite on each side of it (Fig. 21D) and a piece of chrysocolla both above and below it (Fig. 21E). Put malachite over the heart light center (Fig. 21B) with a piece of green fluorite on each side (Fig. 21F) and a piece of purple fluorite both above and below it (Fig. 21G). Center turquoise over the throat center (Fig. 21H) between two pieces of green tourmaline (Fig. 21I). The brow chakra is stimulated by amethyst (Fig. 21J) between moss agate pieces (Fig. 21K), and the crown by amber (Fig. 21L) between pieces of lapis lazuli (Fig. 21M).

Calming Nervous Energy

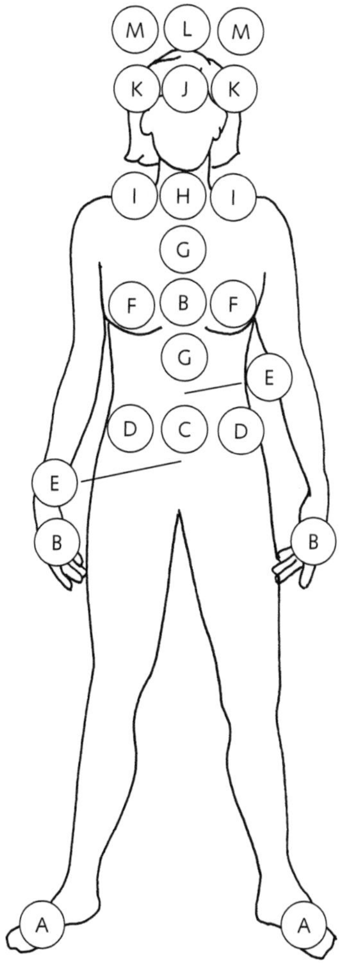

Figure 21

Depression

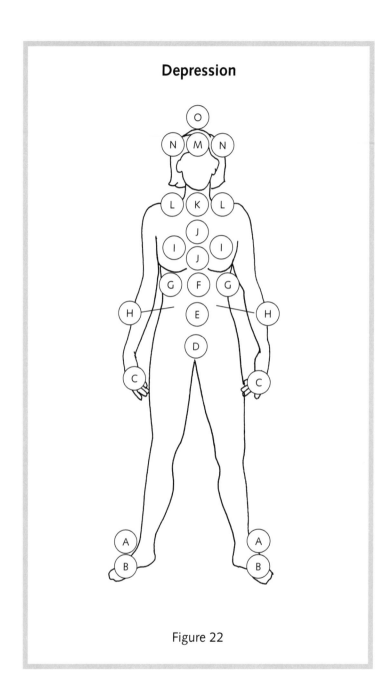

Figure 22

Depression

Stones needed: two moss agate, two orange and brown agate, one turquoise, two chrysocolla, two amber, one amethyst, one carnelian, one chrysoprase, two watermelon tourmaline, two green fluorite, one garnet, one rose quartz, two lapis lazuli, two malachite, two green tourmaline.

Depression can have many causes, including a streak of bad luck, a physical loss, illness, and actual mental troubles. The first thing to do is work on the internal fears of the patient, by using moss agate, orange and brown agate, turquoise, and chrysocolla. Amber is helpful in changing negative attitudes to positive ones, and in dispelling suicidal thoughts. Apply green fluorite to release emotional traumas and use chrysoprase and watermelon tourmaline to heal them. Amethyst will balance the entire aura and soothe mental distress. Lapis lazuli and carnelian are valuable for dispelling apathy and negative thoughts, a side effect of depression. Apply red garnet and rose quartz to ease the depression and create a renewed interest in life. Malachite will further balance the entire physical body system, while green tourmaline will detoxify the aura and chakras.

Begin by placing green tourmaline (Fig. 22A) and orange and brown agate (Fig. 22B) near the sole of each foot and lapis lazuli in the palm of each hand (Fig. 22C). Garnet goes over the root chakra (Fig. 22D), carnelian on the spleen center (Fig. 22E), and rose quartz on the heart area (Fig. 22F). On each side of the rose quartz place malachite (Fig. 22G) and below that moss agate (Fig. 22H). Just above this put two pieces of green fluorite side by side (Fig. 22I); amber goes both above and below the fluorite stones (Fig. 22J). Center chrysoprase on the throat light center (Fig. 22K) between two pieces of watermelon tourmaline (Fig. 22L). Turquoise goes on the brow (Fig. 22M) with a piece of chrysocolla on each side (Fig. 22N). Finish by placing amethyst near the crown chakra (Fig. 22 O).

Broken Bones

Stones needed: one amber, two turquoise, two chrysocolla, one garnet, three lapis lazuli, two malachite, two black onyx, two green tourmaline, and two watermelon tourmaline.

In stone healing it does not matter if the broken bone is encased in a plaster cast. Stone energy will penetrate a cast just as easily as it does clothing.

Amber and turquoise will calm the patient and, along with lapis lazuli and red garnet, purify the aura and chakras. Black onyx is valuable in reducing stress caused by the injury, while malachite will heal and balance the entire system.

Position both malachite (Fig. 23A) and black onyx (Fig. 23B) near the sole of each foot and lapis lazuli in the palm of each hand (Fig. 23C). Garnet goes on the root chakra (Fig. 23D), chrysocolla on the spleen center (Fig. 23E), and watermelon tourmaline over the heart chakra (Fig. 23F). Put green tourmaline on the throat (Fig. 23G) and more lapis lazuli on the brow (Fig. 23H). Amber is situated near the crown chakra (Fig. 23I) between two pieces of turquoise (Fig. 23J).

Figure 23 is an example of treating a broken femur. Place the following stones directly over the broken bone: chrysocolla (Fig. 23K) for internal healing, green tourmaline (Fig. 23L) to alter negative cell structure, and watermelon tourmaline (Fig. 23M) to heal on the cellular level.

Broken Bones

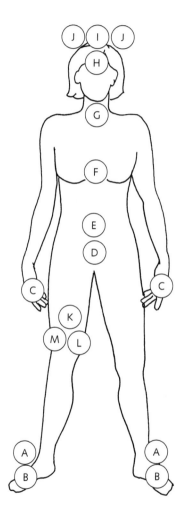

Figure 23

Hysterectomy

Stones needed: two chrysocolla, three amber, two amethyst, two carnelian, one garnet, two chrysoprase, one green fluorite, two hematite, three lapis lazuli, and two malachite.

A hysterectomy not only can be painful and both physically and hormonally disruptive, but also extremely unbalancing, mentally and emotionally, for a woman. If at least one ovary has been left in place, use carnelian and red garnet to strengthen it. If a total hysterectomy was performed, work instead on physical healing and mental rebalancing. Amber will purify the entire system, while amethyst will greatly help with the pain. Hematite is valuable to eliminate any possibility of internal bleeding. Apply lapis lazuli to rebalance and purify the chakras and aura. Green fluorite is good for easing the emotional trauma and chrysoprase for strengthening all the endocrine glands and balancing the mental attitudes. Malachite, placed directly over the incision or pelvic area, will regenerate and heal.

Begin by placing malachite near the sole of each foot (Fig. 24A) and amber in the palm of each hand (Fig. 24B). Directly where the legs join the torso put a piece of carnelian on each side (Fig. 24C). Garnet goes on the root chakra (Fig. 24D) with chrysocolla on each side (Fig. 24E). Immediately above this position two pieces of hematite (Fig. 24F) flanked on each side with a piece of amethyst (Fig. 24G). Just above the hematite place green fluorite (Fig. 24H). Chrysoprase goes on both the heart center and throat chakra (Fig. 24I). Lapis lazuli is placed on the brow and on each side (Fig. 24J) of the amber at the crown of the head (Fig. 24B).

Hysterectomy

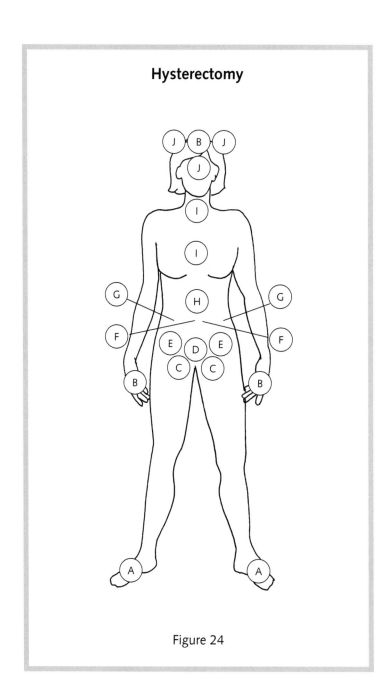

Figure 24

Mastectomy & Breast Problems

Stones needed: three amber, two amethyst, two lapis lazuli, two black obsidian, and two chrysocolla.

A mastectomy, the possibility of one, or any type of breast problem is very stressful and fearful to anyone (female or male). Use amethyst to relieve pain and tension and amber to cleanse and purify the aura and chakras, as well as the body. Lapis lazuli also will clean and balance the chakras and aura. Black obsidian near the sole of each foot will absorb any negative vibrations. Chrysocolla can be placed directly over the breast to accelerate internal healing.

To provide a strong healing flow of energy through the body with the negatives strained out, put black obsidian near the sole of each foot (Fig. 25A) and amber near the crown of the head (Fig. 25B). Place lapis lazuli in each palm (Fig. 25C). Directly over the each breast arrange a piece of chrysocolla (Fig. 25D), above it amethyst (Fig. 25E), and above that amber (Fig. 25B).

Mastectomy & Breast Problems

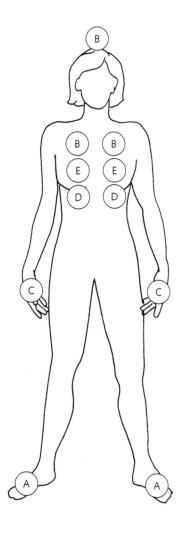

Figure 25

Arthritis

Stones needed: one amethyst, one carnelian, one chrysocolla, one garnet, two lapis lazuli, two malachite, two green tourmaline, and two watermelon tourmaline.

This disease of the joints can be helped by applying carnelian, chrysocolla, and red garnet directly to the inflamed areas (Fig. 26C, G, H). However, arthritis also affects the blood, filling the system with an overload of toxins. For this use green tourmaline and amethyst; amethyst will also aid in relieving pain. The aura and chakras will need to be rebalanced and cleansed, so use green tourmaline and lapis lazuli. Malachite is valuable for rebalancing the entire physical body system and causing regeneration. Watermelon tourmaline will hasten cellular regeneration of damaged joints. Carnelian and chrysocolla can be placed directly on each diseased joint.

Begin the healing by putting green tourmaline at the sole of each foot (Fig. 26A) and lapis lazuli in the palm of each hand (Fig. 26B). Garnet goes on the root chakra (Fig. 26C) and watermelon tourmaline on the heart center (Fig. 26D). On each side of the watermelon tourmaline should be placed a piece of malachite (Fig. 26E). Amethyst is situated near the crown chakra at the top of the head (Fig. 26F).

Arthritis

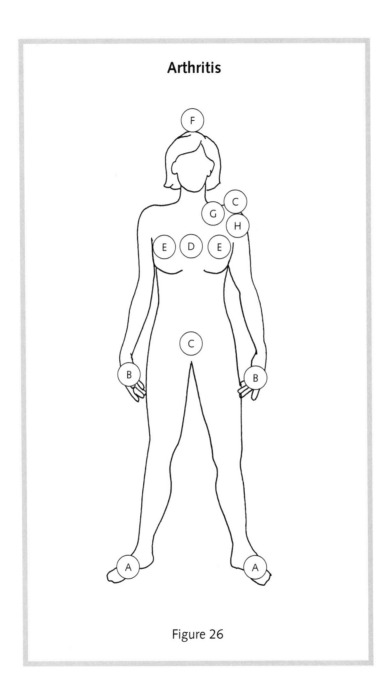

Figure 26

Liver & Gall Bladder Diseases

Stones needed: one carnelian, two malachite, three amethyst, two green tourmaline, one watermelon tourmaline, and two amber.

Although a person can live without a gall bladder, no one can live without a liver. Dietary and lifestyle changes must occur along with the medical and stone healing, or the patient will not recover.

Amber, carnelian, and malachite will be valuable in purifying the entire system, an absolute necessity in treating this disease. Malachite is also useful in purifying, regenerating cell tissue, and rebalancing the entire system. To clean the blood and help relieve pain, apply amethyst. The body will also need to be detoxified and the negative cell structure altered; use green tourmaline for this. To heal on a cellular level, apply watermelon tourmaline.

Green tourmaline is placed near the sole of each foot (Fig. 27A) and amber in the palm of each hand (Fig. 27B). Watermelon tourmaline is situated over the heart chakra (Fig. 27C) and amethyst near the crown of the head (Fig. 27D). On the right side of the patient's abdomen place a piece of carnelian (Fig. 27E) with two pieces of malachite (Fig. 27F) to the left (your left) of that and two pieces of amethyst to the right (Fig. 27D).

Liver & Gall Bladder Diseases

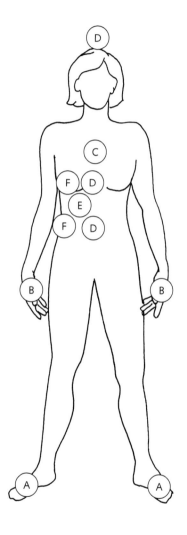

Figure 27

Tumors, Cancerous & Benign

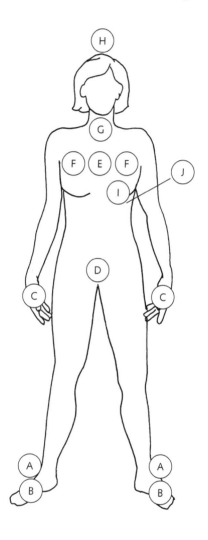

Figure 28

Tumors, Cancerous & Benign

Stones needed: two amber, one amethyst, one chrysocolla, one chrysoprase, one lapis lazuli, two malachite, one turquoise, one pyrite, two rose quartz, and two green tourmaline.

This stone pattern for healing can be used before and after the tumor is removed. When used before, it helps prepare the patient's body to better handle the trauma of surgery and anesthetic. When used afterward, it accelerates healing of the physical, mental, and emotional bodies. Tumors are often encapsulated bits of negative karma, so use amber to purify the aura and chakras as well as promote karmic release. Amethyst will relieve pain, cleanse the blood, and ease worry, while chrysoprase strengthens all the endocrine glands, a necessary factor in fighting off tumors. Malachite and turquoise will regenerate damaged tissue and absorb negative energies. Lapis lazuli purifies, and pyrite uplifts the spirits, making healing easier. Specifically for cancer and internal healing, use chrysocolla. Rose quartz on the heart chakra will help heal the emotional hurts. To detoxify the entire aura and alter negative cell structure, apply green tourmaline. Chrysoprase and chrysocolla may be placed directly over the tumor site. See Figure 28I, J, as an example.

Both malachite (Fig. 28A) and green tourmaline (Fig. 28B) should be placed near the sole of each foot. Put amber in the palm of each hand (Fig. 28C) and lapis lazuli over the root chakra (Fig. 28D). On the heart center, arrange the pyrite (Fig. 28E) with rose quartz on each side of it (Fig. 28F). Turquoise is placed on the throat center (Fig. 28G) and amethyst near the crown of the head (Fig. 28H).

Releasing Emotional Traumas
(Including Incest & Abuse Recovery)

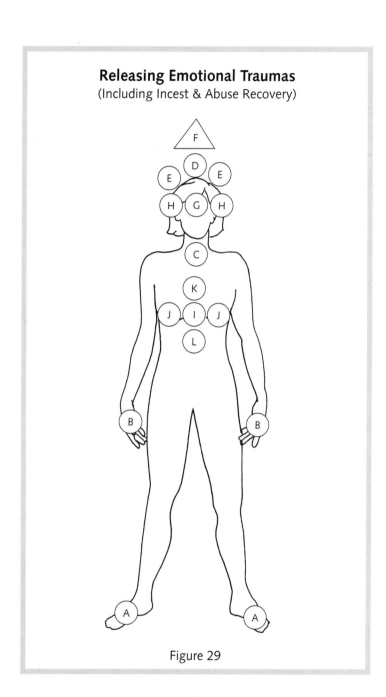

Figure 29

Releasing Emotional Traumas
(Including Incest & Abuse Recovery)

Stones needed: one amber, one chrysocolla, one chrysoprase, two lapis lazuli, one rose quartz, one malachite, two black onyx, two pyrite, two green tourmaline, two watermelon tourmaline, one turquoise, and one clear quartz crystal.

Although professional counseling is extremely valuable in recovering from incest and abuse, stone healing will help the patient release the deep emotional hurts, a necessary part of emotional and mental healing.

Chrysocolla, chrysoprase, lapis lazuli, and rose quartz are particularly valuable for this type of a healing. Amber will purify the aura, while black onyx helps in releasing all negative emotions. Malachite will not only absorb any remaining negatives, it will also bring up any buried feelings so that they, too, can be expelled. Watermelon tourmaline over the heart chakra will heal the love loss often associated with this disease, while turquoise will release the self-guilt that often accompanies it. Apply green tourmaline to balance the lower chakras with the upper ones.

Place black onyx near the sole of each foot (Fig. 29A) and green tourmaline in the palm of each hand (Fig. 29B). Malachite goes on the throat chakra (Fig. 29C) and amber (Fig. 29D), flanked by pyrite (Fig. 29E), at the crown center on top of the head. At the transpersonal point above the crown (Fig. 29F), arrange a clear quartz crystal point. Put turquoise in the center of the forehead (Fig. 29G) with a piece of watermelon tourmaline on each side (Fig. 29H). Directly over the heart chakra arrange rose quartz (Fig. 29I). On each side of this stone place a piece of lapis lazuli (Fig. 29J). Above the rose quartz put chrysocolla (Fig. 29K), and below it place chrysoprase (Fig. 29L).

Diabetes & Hypoglycemia
(Diseases of the Pancreas)

Stones needed: two orange and brown agate, one garnet, two lapis lazuli, three amber, two chrysoprase, two watermelon tourmaline, two malachite, two green tourmaline, one carnelian, and one amethyst.

Diabetes and hypoglycemia are opposite ends of the same disease and are very often associated with a lack of love at some time in the patient's life, usually in childhood.

Orange and brown agate, red garnet, and lapis lazuli will help to purify the blood. Amethyst, carnelian, and malachite are specifically associated with this disease and aid other stones in the healing. To clean the entire system and strengthen the endocrine glands, apply amber, chrysoprase, and watermelon tourmaline. Finally, use green tourmaline to detoxify the aura and chakras.

Start the detoxification flow through the body by placing green tourmaline near the sole of each foot (Fig. 30A). Garnet goes on the root center (Fig. 30B) with a piece of lapis lazuli on each side of it (Fig. 30C). Immediately above that put carnelian (Fig. 30D). Above the carnelian goes a piece of amber (Fig. 30E), followed by two pieces of chrysoprase (Fig. 30F). Above this, place two pieces of orange and brown agate (Fig. 30G), and then another piece of amber (Fig. 30E). Two pieces of malachite should go on the throat chakra (Fig. 30F). Center a piece of amber on the brow (Fig. 30E), flanked on each side by watermelon tourmaline (Fig. 30G). Amethyst goes near the crown chakra (Fig. 30H).

Diabetes & Hypoglycemia
(Diseases of the Pancreas)

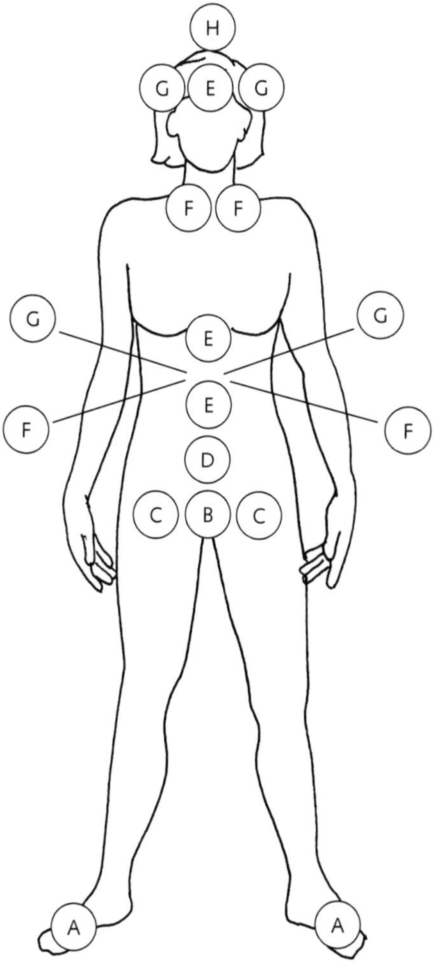

Figure 30

Drug & Alcohol Recovery

Stones needed: one amethyst, two amber, one tiger's-eye, two chrysoprase, one green fluorite, two purple fluorite, two hematite, two lapis lazuli, two malachite, one rose quartz, two green tourmaline, and two clear quartz crystals.

In drug and alcohol recovery, there is no quick fix. The patient must absolutely seek counseling and be actively committed to her/his recovery. If she/he is not, the healer should not attempt a stone healing; it will not work.

Stones associated specifically with this type of healing are amethyst, amber, and tiger's-eye. Calm the nerves with green fluorite and stabilize the aura with purple fluorite. Hematite will reduce stress and chrysoprase will bring inner peace. Green tourmaline can cleanse and purify the blood. Lapis lazuli also can cleanse the aura and chakras and protect against negative energies. Malachite is used to absorb negative influences, while rose quartz over the heart chakra will develop a feeling of oneness with all life. To detoxify the aura and chakras, apply green tourmaline.

Malachite goes near the sole of each foot (Fig. 31A) and hematite in the palm of each hand (Fig. 31B). Place a piece of green tourmaline on each side of the body, flanking the spleen chakra (Fig. 31C). At the heart center put rose quartz (Fig. 31D) with lapis lazuli on each side (Fig. 31E), purple fluorite below (Fig. 31F), and green fluorite above it (Fig. 31G). Center tiger's-eye on the forehead (Fig. 31H) and put a piece of chrysoprase on each side (Fig. 31I). At the crown of the head arrange amethyst (Fig. 31J) flanked on each side by amber (Fig. 31K). Place a clear quartz crystal point below the feet and another above the head at the transpersonal point (Fig. 31L).

Drug and Alcohol Recovery

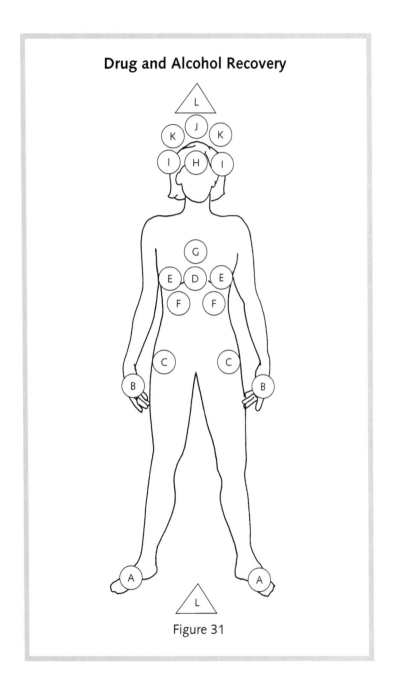

Figure 31

Pregnancy & Childbirth

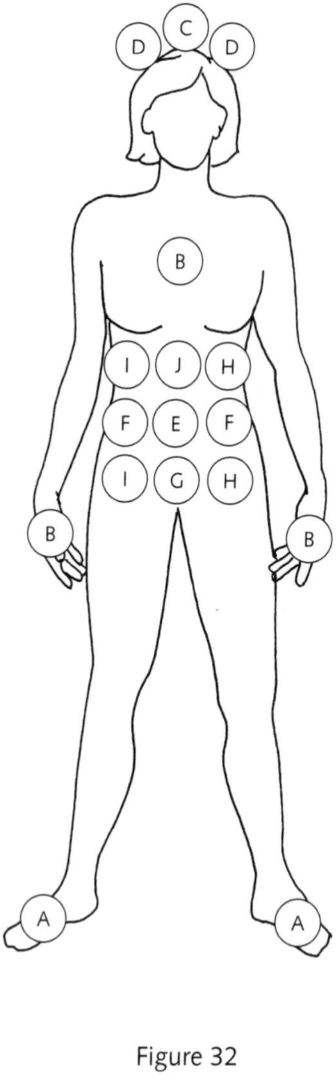

Figure 32

Pregnancy & Childbirth

Stones needed: two orange and brown agate, one chrysocolla, one chrysoprase, two brown agate, one amethyst, one garnet, two hematite, three rose quartz, two green tourmaline, and two turquoise.

This stone healing is not for the woman who wants to become pregnant, but for one who already is or is ready to give birth. Orange and brown agate, chrysocolla, and chrysoprase are particularly useful in an overall sense when working for a healthy pregnancy and easy labor and birth. Brown agate will help with nausea, while turquoise will calm, balance, and absorb any surrounding negative energies. Rose quartz placed over the heart chakra will build a sense of oneness between the mother and child. Amethyst is useful in cleansing and balancing the aura; it can help to lessen pain during labor. Detoxify the aura and chakras with green tourmaline, thus creating a more positive atmosphere for both mother and baby. When labor begins, or is very near, red garnet will strengthen the mother, and hematite will keep bleeding under control.

Put green tourmaline near the sole of each foot (Fig. 32A) and rose quartz in the palm of each hand (Fig. 32B). Rose quartz also goes on the heart chakra (Fig. 32B), while amethyst (Fig. 32C), flanked on both sides by turquoise (Fig. 32D), goes near the crown of the head. Over the abdomen, center a piece of garnet (Fig. 32E), flanked on each side by brown agate (Fig. 32F). Directly below the garnet put a piece of chrysoprase (Fig. 32G) with orange and brown agate on the right (your right) side (Fig. 32H) and hematite on the left (Fig. 32I). Above the garnet position a piece of chrysocolla (Fig. 32J) with orange and brown agate on the right side of the patient's body (Fig. 32H) and hematite on the left (Fig. 32I). You may wish to place several clear quartz crystals around the body.

High Blood Pressure

Stones needed: three amber, one amethyst, two green fluorite, one turquoise, one lapis lazuli, two hematite, two chrysocolla, and four green tourmaline.

A patient with high blood pressure should immediately seek medical aid and follow specific dietary changes in order to bring this disease under control. Combine standard treatment with stone healing to lessen the symptoms and aid healing in general.

Lapis lazuli and green tourmaline are specific stones for this disease, in addition to green tourmaline's ability to detoxify the aura and chakras. Ease tension by applying chrysocolla, and calm and balance the entire body through the use of amethyst, green fluorite, hematite, and turquoise. Amber will purify the entire physical body system.

Arrange green tourmaline near the sole of each foot (Fig. 33A) and amber in each palm and at the crown chakra (Fig. 33B). Over the heart, center place a piece of lapis lazuli (Fig. 33C) with green tourmaline on each side of it (Fig. 34A) and chrysocolla above and below it (Fig. 33D). Put turquoise on the throat center (Fig. 33E), flanked on each side with a piece of hematite (Fig. 33F). In the center of the brow, place amethyst (Fig. 33G) with green fluorite on each side (Fig. 33H).

High Blood Pressure

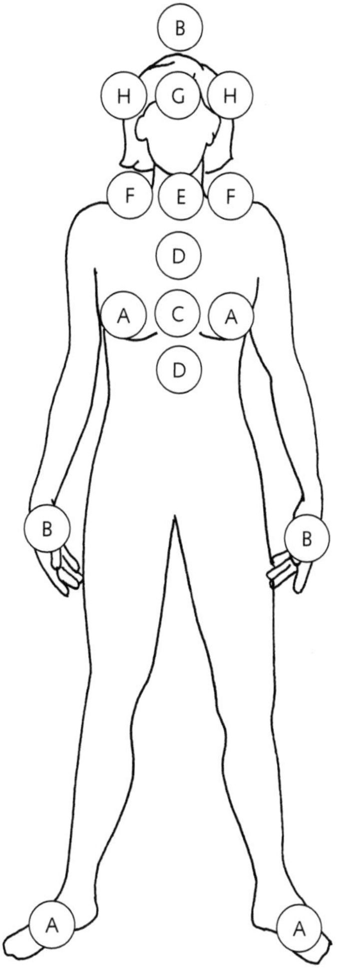

Figure 33

Past-Life Cleansing

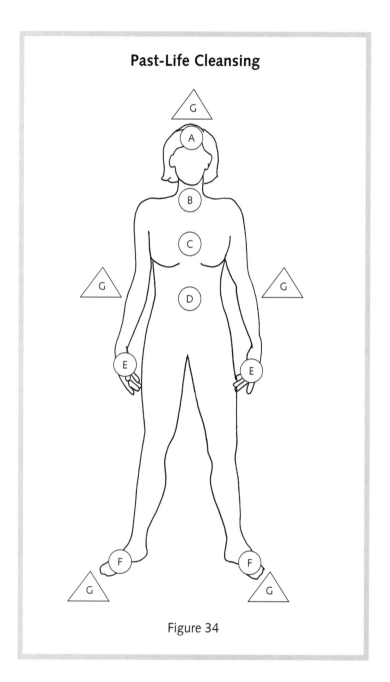

Figure 34

Past-Life Cleansing

This stone-healing pattern is often necessary when nothing else seems to work well. It really does not matter if the present problems arose from the past of this life or from past lives of other times. Each of us carries hundreds of old tapes in our subconscious and superconscious minds: tapes of events, deeds, and/or habit patterns that can surface at any time in this life to create havoc and disease without our willing them to do so.

When using this pattern, some patients will find themselves watching or reliving old experiences or past lives without warning. Be alert for any sign of distress or discomfort, ending the healing session quickly if the person becomes agitated or nervous.

This healing pattern is to release any lingering effects of any past life. The patient needs this release so that healing can take place, whatever the root cause of the problem. After the patient is lying down, and before you arrange the stones, instruct her/him to immediately release any negative emotions or remembrances as soon as they come into her/his mind. One way to do this is to have the patient visualize her/himself dropping the negative images into a deep well.

Stones needed: one lapis lazuli for the brow (Fig. 34A); one turquoise for the throat (Fig. 34B); one watermelon tourmaline for the heart (Fig. 34C); one rose quartz for the abdomen (Fig. 34D); one amber for the palm of each hand (Fig. 34E); and one black obsidian to be placed near the sole of each foot (Fig. 34F); and five large, clear quartz crystals for the outer pattern (Fig. 34G).

Lapis lazuli not only purifies and balances all the chakras, it gives the wisdom necessary to understand past lives and helps to release emotional pain caused by past events. Turquoise is a master healing stone. It is valuable for balancing, grounding, absorbing negatives, and protecting. Watermelon tourmaline balances the lower chakras with the upper ones, enabling the patient to transform the energy of past negative events into positive ones. Rose quartz soothes and calms, heals deep emotional wounds, and brings inner peace. Amber makes it possible to release karmic ties by purifying the entire system, aura, and chakras. Black obsidian is important for its grounding and stabilizing energy. It also enables the patient to make contact with the Akashic records on the astral.

Position the body stones first, then the outer pattern of crystal points as follows.

The outer pattern of quartz crystals is activated in the form of a five-point star. Begin by tapping the crystal near the patient's right foot, then the one over the head, down to the left foot, up to the crystal near the right hand, across to the one by the left hand, and back to the crystal at the right foot. Tap the crystals in the same sequence in which you laid them out.

Although this stone pattern is a powerful aid for most people, it must be used with care and consideration of the patient's mental and emotional stability. If the patient is extremely nervous or suffering from any type of mental problem, this pattern is not recommended.

CHAPTER V

Stone Patterns for Magic

Stones can be used in all kinds of magical spellworking, either directly on a physical body, a photograph, or even on a list of accomplishments you wish to manifest. The same ethics apply to all magic: never use this power to harm or control another person. You are responsible and will build karma (good or bad) for your actions. Think carefully before doing magic; as you are very likely to get what you spell for.

Any of the following magical stone patterns can be used in conjunction with ritual, candle burning, divination with cards or other tools, or meditation. Any of the stone patterns worked directly on a physical body can also be used on a photograph of yourself or another person. Setting the stones and photo on an altar or under a pyramid will intensify the power aimed at your goal. Burning a seven-day white candle near a stone pattern on a photo will also intensify the power as will burning a magenta candle. Sometimes laying the quartz crystals so that their points are aimed at the photo will increase the manifestation rate.

By reading about the powers of the stones in chapter 6, you can devise any number of additional stone patterns for magic.

Releasing Karmic Ties

Stones needed: one moss agate, two amber, two black obsidian, one amethyst, four carnelian, two chrysocolla, two black onyx, one chrysoprase, two lapis lazuli, two malachite, and two watermelon tourmaline.

Moss agate is for enlightenment and contacting the spirit guides. Amethyst helps you open to the spiritual, which is the realm in which you find those guides. Tiger's-eye aids in recognizing the karmic ties, black obsidian is valuable in dealing with them, and amber is important for karmic release. Use malachite to discover buried feelings connected with these ties. Black onyx not only helps in making psychic contact but also absorbs negative vibrations. Another stone for seeing into the past is carnelian. Chrysocolla is valuable for releasing anger, grief, and tension associated with karmic ties, while chrysoprase will help with the emotional healing as does watermelon tourmaline. Balance the aura and chakras through the use of lapis lazuli.

Begin by placing black onyx (Fig. 35A) and chrysocolla (Fig. 35B) near the sole of each foot and amber in the palm of each hand (Fig. 35C). Chrysoprase goes over the heart chakra (Fig. 35D), flanked on each side by a piece of malachite (Fig. 35E). Arrange a piece of watermelon tourmaline (Fig. 35F) both above and below the chrysoprase. At the throat center, place moss agate (Fig. 35G) with lapis lazuli on either side (Fig. 35H). Above each eyebrow place two pieces of carnelian (Fig. 35I). Amethyst goes near the crown of the head (Fig. 35J) between two pieces of black obsidian (Fig. 35K).

Releasing Karmic Ties

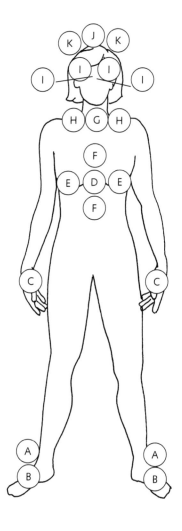

Figure 35

Attracting a True Love

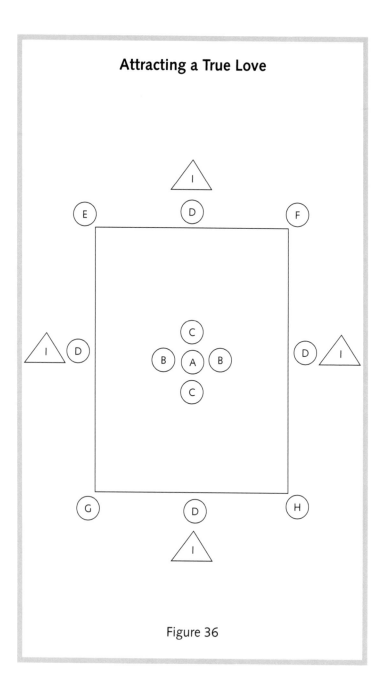

Figure 36

Attracting a True Love

Stones needed: one rose quartz, two garnet, four green tourmaline, two watermelon tourmaline, one amethyst, one chrysocolla, one lapis lazuli, one pyrite, and four clear quartz crystals.

Never do any spellwork in an attempt to deliberately make a specific person love you! This will not gain you the perfect love for your life; it will only bring you a karmic debt that will be difficult and painful to discharge. If you have had several negative relationships that ended in emotional pain or physical fear, you obviously are not making good choices. Turn the matter over to your spiritual teachers and let them bring the right person to you.

Rose quartz, red garnet, green tourmaline, and watermelon tourmaline are very helpful in drawing the appropriate true love to you. Amethyst will help break negative patterns, personal habits that got you in trouble before when you chose the wrong person or walked away from the right one. Chrysocolla will help to eliminate the fear of commitment and to open yourself to another. Lapis lazuli is important for balancing the chakras and aura, making it possible for good things to come to you, while pyrite will uplift sagging self-esteem and confidence.

You will need to use a photo of yourself for this magical pattern, as you will want to leave it active for a period of time. Place the photo where it will not be disturbed until you are ready to dismantle it. You may put a pyramid over it if you wish.

Begin by placing a piece of rose quartz on the center of the photo (Fig. 36A). On each side of the rose quartz place a piece of red garnet (Fig. 36B). Above and below the quartz, place watermelon tourmaline (Fig. 36C). At the edges of the center of each side, put green tourmaline (Fig. 36D). At the upper left corner, put amethyst (Fig. 36E) and at the upper right, pyrite (Fig. 36F). At the lower left corner place chrysocolla (Fig. 36G) and at the lower right lapis lazuli (Fig. 36H). Activate the energy flow by placing a clear quartz crystal point at each of the fours sides (Fig. 36I), with the points all in one direction.

Enhancing Psychic Abilities

Stones needed: one moss agate, one amethyst, two purple fluorite, three lapis lazuli, two black obsidian, two black onyx, two turquoise, one garnet, and two malachite.

To strengthen your intuitive hunches and open to other psychic talents, you need to develop not only your connections with the astral realm, but gain more confidence in your ability and right to use these talents. Moss agate will help to communicate with the spiritual guides and teachers. The third eye in the center of the forehead is stimulated by red garnet, while malachite, which strengthens the tie between the seen and the unseen, will aid in developing your intuition. Other stones that will help are amethyst, purple fluorite, lapis lazuli, black obsidian, black onyx, and turquoise.

Put black obsidian (Fig. 37A) and black onyx (Fig. 37B) near the sole of each foot. Over the heart chakra goes a piece of moss agate (Fig. 37C), flanked on each side by lapis lazuli (Fig. 37D). Arrange another piece of lapis lazuli on the throat chakra (Fig. 37D) with turquoise on each side (Fig. 37E). Stimulate the third eye by placing red garnet on it (Fig. 37F); two pieces of malachite goes directly above the garnet (Fig. 37G). At the crown of the head position an amethyst (Fig. 37H) flanked by purple fluorite (Fig. 37I).

Enhancing Psychic Abilities

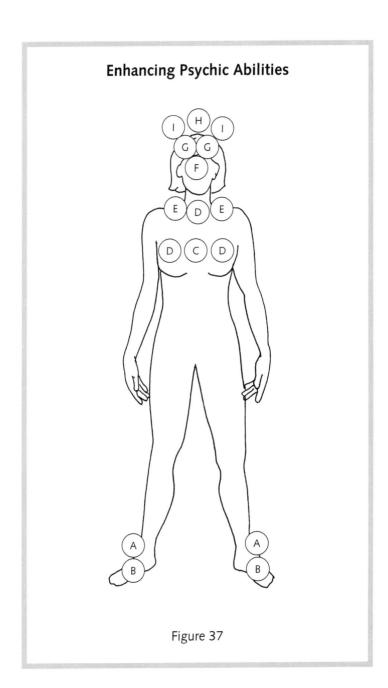

Figure 37

Protection Against Psychic Attack

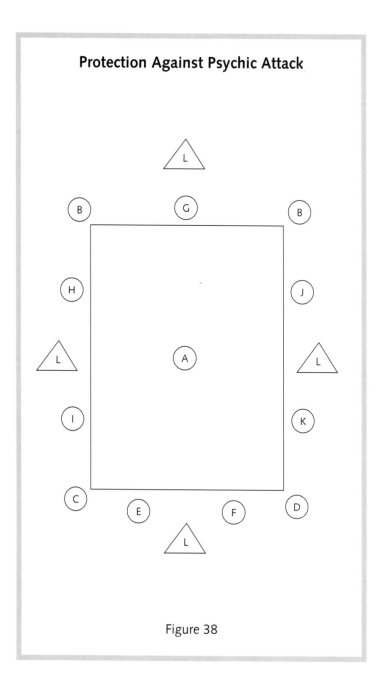

Figure 38

Protection Against Psychic Attack

Stones needed: one moss agate, one carnelian, one garnet, one malachite, one amber, two lapis lazuli, one black obsidian, one black onyx, one pyrite, one tiger's-eye, one turquoise, and four clear quartz crystals.

Many people think that someone must actively do black magic to produce a psychic attack against another person. However, this is not true. A jealous or vindictive person who wishes you ill can affect you in small ways, which build up eventually to an avalanche of bad luck and misfortune. It is best not to name a specific person when working to clear your aura and atmosphere of psychic attack; you may get the wrong person or miss the mark completely. Keep your request for protection general in nature, aiming only to shield yourself. This leaves the negative psychic energy with nowhere to go except back to the sender. In this manner you build no negative karma for yourself.

Amber and tiger's-eye are excellent for repelling attack and returning it to the sender, while moss agate, carnelian, garnet, and malachite will protect your aura from contamination. Both black obsidian and black onyx will absorb whatever negatives are already within your aura and environment. Use lapis lazuli to balance all your chakras and protect you against further influence. Turquoise will calm and ground you as well as protect. The glittering stone pyrite also protects and uplifts your outlook on life.

Since you will want to leave this stone pattern for some time, place the stones over a photo of yourself, your family, and/or pets. Place the photo where it will not be disturbed until you wish to dismantle it. You can place a pyramid over it if you wish.

Put a piece of turquoise in the center of the photo (Fig. 38A).

At the two upper corners place lapis lazuli (Fig. 38B), at the bottom left corner black onyx (Fig. 38C), and the bottom right corner black obsidian (Fig. 38D). Put a piece of pyrite (Fig. 38E) and a piece of tiger's-eye (Fig. 38F) between the bottom stones, and a piece of amber between the top stones (Fig. 38G). Along the left side put moss agate near the top (Fig. 38H) and malachite near the bottom (Fig. 38I). On the right side place carnelian near the top (Fig. 38J) and garnet near the bottom (Fig. 38K). Activate the stone pattern by placing a small clear quartz crystal point at each side of the photo (Fig. 38L).

Drawing Prosperity & Good Luck

Stones needed: four hematite, four pyrite, two tiger's-eye, one green tourmaline, two watermelon tourmaline, and four clear quartz crystals.

Everyone desires more prosperity and good luck, which you can attract by creating positive changes for your life. You will need hematite to help you focus your energy and pyrite to boost your self-confidence. Tiger's-eye will build optimism and willpower, while watermelon tourmaline increases your creative ideas. Green tourmaline not only attracts prosperity, but also is valuable in manifesting the things you desire.

This is another magical stone pattern you will want to leave active for some time. Place a photo of yourself where it will not be disturbed until you are ready to deactivate it by removing the stones. You may place a pyramid over it if you wish.

Place green tourmaline in the center of the photo (Fig. 39A), flanked on each side and above and below it by a piece of hematite (Fig. 39B). Put watermelon tourmaline in the center of the top and bottom edges (Fig. 39C), with tiger's-eye in the center of both side edges (Fig. 39D). A piece of pyrite goes at

Drawing Prosperity & Good Luck

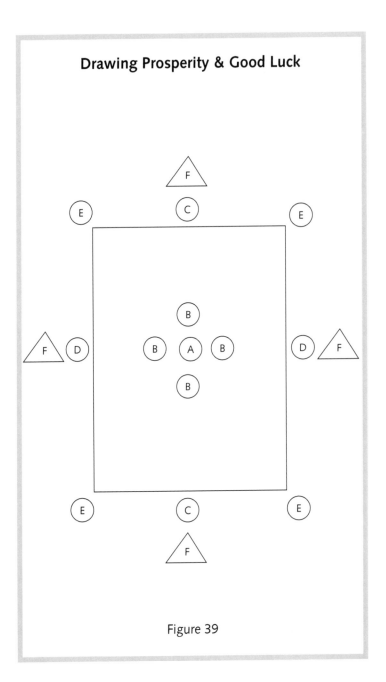

Figure 39

each of the four corners (Fig. 39E). Activate the energy flow by placing a clear quartz crystal point at each of the four sides of the photo (Fig. 39F).

Learning About Past Lives

Stones needed: one moss agate, one lapis lazuli, two purple fluorite, one amethyst, one garnet, two malachite, two carnelian, two black obsidian, two black onyx, and two clear quartz crystals.

The very last reason you should seek to know your past lives is to discover if you were someone famous. Logically, few people will have been an important historical figure. Those types of people did not produce the culture in which they lived, they were its product. Culture and history were created by ordinary people: people who produced the crops and crafts, had families, protected their country, and demanded justice from those over them. The only reasons for accessing your past lives should be constructive ones; for example, a desire to regain talents, to discover why a particular life or person from that life might influence the present, or to avoid repeating mistakes through certain behavior or personal associations.

Moss agate will aid in opening the psychic and bring enlightenment so you can access the Akashic records, the repository of all past lives. Purple fluorite and lapis lazuli will also help in this. To strengthen the third eye in the center of your forehead, use red garnet; the third eye helps one to see into the past. Amethyst will also open you to the spiritual, while malachite both connects the seen (physical) to the unseen (spiritual) and increases the power of psychic sight. Black obsidian and black onyx are valuable for absorbing negative energy and emotions that may arise from viewing these past lives.

Learning About Past Lives

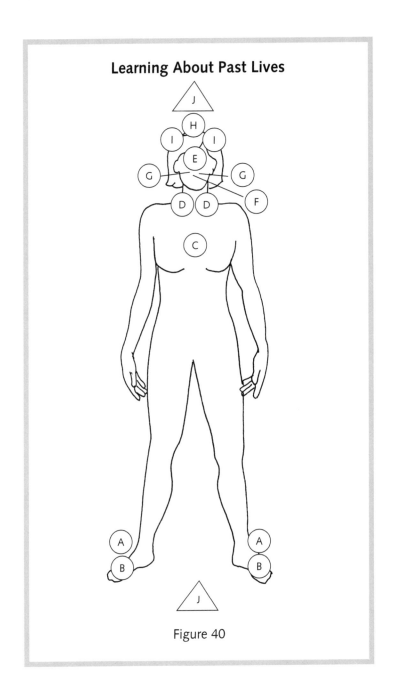

Figure 40

This stone pattern should be placed directly on the body of the person wishing to learn of her/his past lives. To begin, arrange black obsidian (Fig. 40A) and black onyx (Fig. 40B) near the sole of each foot. Lapis lazuli goes over the heart chakra (Fig. 40C), and two pieces of purple fluorite over the throat center (Fig. 40D). Put red garnet in the center of the forehead (Fig. 40E) with a piece of moss agate directly below it (Fig. 40F). On each side of the moss agate, place a piece of malachite (Fig. 40G). Amethyst goes near the crown chakra (Fig. 40H), flanked on each side by carnelian (Fig. 40I). Activate the magical pattern by placing a clear quartz crystal point near the feet and at the transpersonal point above the head (Fig. 40J).

This magical stone pattern may have to be repeated several times before it breaks through the subconscious barrier, which naturally keeps us from being bombarded with past life memories.

CHAPTER VI

Stones & Their Magical Powers

Agate

Agates in general increase strength and courage; they also balance energies.

Blue Lace Agate works well on the throat, heart, brow, and crown chakras. It is used for problems such as laryngitis, sore throat, hoarseness, arthritis, hereditary bone deformity, breaks, and fractures; it is also used for general strengthening of the bones, the fingernails and toenails, digestion, the glands, and the eyes. It will calm and soothe the nervous system, as well as remove blockages.

Moss Agate opens the crown and brow chakras and connects the physical to the spiritual. It can protect the aura, cleanse the environment, and balance logic with intuition. Its many uses include bringing enlightenment, inducing calmness, drawing luck, aiding meditation, opening the psychic, learning divination, creating inner peace, establishing connectedness, visiting the astral realms, aiding visualization, feeling universal and healing love, contacting the spiritual guides, assisting agricultural fertility, reducing fevers, dispelling fear, encouraging sobriety and chastity, improving the self-esteem, attracting prosperity, and drawing new ideas. In healing it is good for conception, the eyes, fungal infections, eliminating toxins from the body, colds, flu, internal infections, and skin disorders.

Brown Agate helps with grounding, indigestion, and nausea. Orange and brown grounds, balances, stabilizes, and protects; it connects with the spleen or belly chakra, and is associated with emotions, childbirth, menstrual cramps, stomach diseases, dispelling fear, preventing falls, teething, hearing, the heart, the blood, fevers, and epilepsy.

Amber

This stone resonates with the brain wave patterns and can change negativity to positiveness. This organic stone should never be cleaned with salt or salt water. An aura healer, it cleans and purifies the entire system on all levels and opens the crown chakra. It soothes, calms, protects, enables karmic release, repels psychic attacks, lessens the damage of anesthetics, helps in making choices, balances the electromagnetics of the physical body, and gently revitalizes when you are depleted or stressed. It is useful for treating the digestive system, the endocrine glands, the liver, asthma, infection, pain, hysteria, depression, suicidal tendencies, birth, the throat, goiter, the kidneys and bladder, and for drawing out negativity. Golden/yellow amber matches the solar plexus chakra and restores yin/yang balance. Use it for protection, calm, infections, the ears, vision, ulcers, bleeding, the teeth, pain, stabilization, amputations, the lungs, the skin, the hair, asthma, the urinary tract and intestines, poisoning, and the throat.

In the magical procedures previously listed, any color of amber will work well, as it combines with the energies of other stones and produces the correct balance needed.

Amethyst

A major stabilizing and grounding stone, amethyst balances the aura, transforms, cleanses, brings peace and strength, repels psychic attack, helps manage responsibilities, aligns the astral bodies, improves meditation, and breaks negative patterns. It can transmute lower energy into higher energy and cleanse the aura. Use it for pain control, mental problems, blood cleansing, headaches, migraine, insomnia, stress, sedation, calmness, meditation, the nerves, tension, diabetes, the lungs, the eyes, asthma, allergies, the sinuses, nightmares, gout, blood clots, anger, grief, burnout, worry, hearing disorders, bone strength, the endocrine glands, the nervous system, digestion, the heart, the stomach, the skin, the teeth, headaches, insomnia, mental disorders, arthritis, and handling the issue of death. On the spiritual levels, this stone helps with developing the psychic abilities, concentration, creativity, and opening to the spiritual.

Bloodstone

This stone brings renewal, revitalization, practical guidance, wisdom, harmony, helps with decision making, improves meditation, accesses universal love, enhances talents and creativity, and facilitates contacting deceased ancestors. In healing, use it for bladder problems, bleeding, spleen, blood disorders, the kidneys, the bladder, the intestines, the liver, leukemia, eyesight, lung congestion, and rashes. It will neutralize toxins in the body, particularly in the blood, and stabilize the blood flow.

Carnelian

Connected with the belly or spleen chakra, this stone works very well on the first four chakras. It dispels apathy, raises moods, helps with creative visualization, aids in seeing into the past, stimulates the emotions, grounds, and protects. It awakens the talents, draws inspiration, banishes sorrow, increases perception, removes envy, fear or rage, cleanses negative vibrations from other stones, stabilizes the energy in an environment, increases physical energy and creativity, and eliminates psychic attack and ghosts. It is used for healing cuts and abrasions, the pancreas, the spleen, the spine, colds, allergies, kidney stones, gall stones, neuralgia, mental problems, non-inflammatory arthritis, rheumatism, the digestive organs, reproduction, menstrual cramps, the lungs, constipation, the liver, the gall bladder, the ovaries, the testes, joint diseases of all kinds, and allergies.

Chrysocolla

This blue-green stone is connected with both the heart and throat chakras and calms the first three chakras. Like lapis lazuli, it opens all the chakras and builds a connection between the lower chakras and the higher ones. It can remove writer's block, release anger, soothe grief, ease heartache and tension, create better communication, establish grounding, build a link to the Earth spirits, give inner strength, remove stress, purify the environment, rebuild relationships, help with third eye visions and meditation, and balance the emotions. Use it for internal healing of all kinds: fear, sadness, mastectomy, hysterectomy, the lungs, the throat, the heart, cramps, inflammations, the digestive tract, nervousness, headaches, migraines, tension, arthritis, cancer, menstrual cramps, premenstrual syndrome, abortion, birth, anger, fevers, burns, infections, the thyroid, vocal problems, asthma, epilepsy, help irregular production of insulin in the pancreas, blood disorders, tuberculosis, asthma, emphysema, muscle cramps, and incest recovery.

Chrysoprase

This stone balances the attitudes and the yin/yang (or female/male energies), aligns the chakras, promotes an acceptance of one's self, heals heartache, and opens the heart to universal love. In healing, use it for the reproductive organs, fertility, the heart, bleeding, childbirth, the glands, loneliness, inner peace, courage, fear, and old traumas.

Fluorite

Purple and green colors of fluorite are the colors used most by healers and magicians. In general, fluorite can stabilize the mind and emotions, help one see through illusions, restore order, help with concentration, and purify. Use it to heal colds, flu, staph and strep infections, canker sores, herpes, ulcers, infectious diseases, bone structure, and DNA damage.

Green Fluorite releases emotional traumas, calms the nervous system, and renews the chakras. It is good for mild traumas to the emotions, the stomach, the intestinal tract, colitis, heartburn, and sore throat.

Purple Fluorite, a stone of the third eye, aids in psychic development, intuition, meditation, concentration, and mental stability. Use it for grounding, transmuting, calming, protecting, focusing the mind, stroke, nervousness, the bones, stress, insomnia, the brain, epilepsy, Parkinson's disease, and screening out too much empathy.

Garnet, Red

Connected with the root chakra, this stone draws Earth energy, removes negatives from the chakras, balances the kundalini, boosts fertility, draws a compatible mate, opens the third eye, protects against all negatives, gives courage, stimulates the root and crown chakras, regenerates, and stimulates the imagination. Use it for conception, love, happiness, power, strength, possessions, peace, patience, sexuality, balance, cleansing, renewal, birth, menstruation, the blood, arthritis, the sex organs (female or male), depression, rheumatism, and general purification of the body and aura.

Hematite

This gray black stone is connected with the root chakra. Use it for grounding, calming, relaxing, lack of courage, preventing or controlling bleeding and hemorrhage, ulcers, muscle cramps, childbirth, bloodshot eyes, anemia, blood disorders, leg cramps, nervous disorders, insomnia, bone breaks or fractures, kidney and bladder problems, hysteria, high blood pressure, and stress reduction. It also focuses the energy and emotions, balances the yin/yang, enhances the memory, helps to sort out ideas, aids mental attunement and focus, dispels negativity, and balances the emotions.

Lapis Lazuli

Known as an all-healing stone, it is connected with both the brow and throat chakras. It purifies and balances all the chakras and aural layers and gives wisdom to understand spiritual mysteries. It can dispel negativity, energize the throat and brow chakras, expand awareness, attune to creative sources, aid in understanding dreams, strengthen intuition, balance the yin/yang, bring success in relationships, protect from psychic attack, shield and build the aura, raise moods, release past pain, cleanse, protect, and aid in developing the psychic. Use it for infections, pain, fevers, swelling, inflammation, burns, the blood, the heart, throat diseases, the bone marrow, insomnia, dizziness, hearing loss, repairing DNA damage, speech problems, the senses, the nervous system, the spine, calming, insomnia, depression, migraines, purification, incest recovery, prevention of strokes, the eyes, epilepsy, multiple sclerosis, throat congestion, stings, rashes, and high blood pressure.

Malachite

This green stone, which is connected with both the solar plexus and heart chakras, should never be cleaned with salt or salt water. It purifies, regenerates, clears the chakras, stimulates the heart and throat chakras, changes negative situations, releases negative experiences, balances, heals, inspires hope, changes, absorbs negatives, roots out buried feelings and issues, prevents psychic attacks, creates an unobstructed path to goals, builds the intuition, transforms, and heals and balances the entire system. It also connects the seen to the unseen, the physical to spiritual, through the strengthening of the psychic sight. Use it for eye infections, the spleen, the pancreas, asthma, menstrual disorders, poisoning, rheumatism, the liver, the gall bladder, ease in labor, arthritis, swollen joints, tumors, broken bones, torn muscles, the nerves, irregular menstruation, epilepsy, colic, the joints, spasms, purifying the blood, nerve diseases, hypoglycemia, allergies, dyslexia, and enhancing the immune system.

Obsidian, Black

A stone associated with the root chakra, it grounds, centers, stabilizes, calms, protects, absorbs and shields from negative thoughtforms, and collects scattered energies. It is valuable for working on the eyes, acting as a psychic mirror, opening the inner sight, making psychic contact, dealing with past lives, receiving a clear picture of changes needed, astral travel, creativity, and insight into the future. Pair it with clear quartz crystal to diminish fears and illusions.

Onyx, Black

This stone will absorb and release negativity, protect, balance, reduce stress, center and align the chakras and astral bodies, banish grief, enhance self-control, balance the yin/yang, help the memory, draw good fortune, and aid in psychic contact. In healing it is good for the bone marrow and the feet.

Pyrite

This glittering mineral grounds, uplifts the spirits, helps in seeing through illusion, aids the memory and intellect, and protects from negatives. Use it in healing for the bones, the cells, DNA damage, bronchitis, the lungs, infectious diseases, fevers, and inflammations.

Quartz Crystal, Clear

A very powerful, transpersonal stone, it heals, clears, and aligns the body, chakras, and aura. It also detoxifies the aura, cleanses on all levels, helps with clear thinking, aids in contacting spiritual guides, alters states of consciousness, enhances psychic ability, opens the third eye during meditation, speeds healing, energizes, gives clear dreams, and dispels negatives. When placed on the heart chakra, quartz crystal will clear out emotional disturbances and bring harmony. Placed on the crown chakra it activates that light center. In healing, use it for the thyroid and the parathyroid glands, congestion, sore throat, to strengthen the immune system, and to intensify the energy of all other stones used.

Rose Quartz

Associated with the heart chakra, this stone balances, rejuvenates, removes negative energy from the chakras, relieves depression, heals deep emotional hurts, and opens the heart to love and self-love. Use it also for acceptance, a positive outlook, forgiveness, joy, oneness, learning self-love, calming, balancing the yin/yang, healing emotional pain, trust, honesty, aging, inner peace, fear, grief, and recovery from childhood abuse. In healing, rose quartz is useful for releasing cellular impurity, the throat, the ears, the nose, the sinuses, the kidneys, hypertension, palsy, clearing the skin, diminishing pain, the adrenal glands, and relieving stress and tension.

Tiger's-Eye, Golden Brown

Associated with the solar plexus chakra, this stone helps in recognizing karmic ties, aids in manifesting ideas into reality, returns negative energy, protects against psychic attack, grounds, balances, and gives optimism. It also helps with cheering, purifying the system, increasing perception, clarity, understanding and intuition, enhancing the psychic perception, disciplining the emotions, balancing the yin/yang, and stimulating wealth. Use it for the eyes, night vision, the throat, the reproductive organs, broken bones, digestion, drug and alcohol recovery, the will, and intellectual stimulation.

Tourmaline

All types of tourmaline align the chakras, protect, inspire, balance the female/male energies, balance the activity of the right and left sides of the brain, and clear the aura.

Green tourmaline (also called verdelite) is connected with the heart and solar plexus chakras. An all-purpose healer, it balances the lower chakras with the higher ones and can open the heart chakra. It soothes, transforms negative energy, inspires creativity, detoxifies the aura and chakras, draws prosperity and creativity, calms fears, stabilizes the emotions, protects, draws love, and dispels fear and negativity. It is said to alter cell structure also. Use it for weight loss, the liver, the gall bladder, the heart, the ductless glands, the immune system, the nerves and nervous system healing, flu, manifesting, digestion, the intestines, purifying the blood, the veins, constipation, the teeth, the bones, asthma, and high blood pressure.

Watermelon tourmaline is also connected with both the heart and solar plexus chakras. It heals past emotional scars, balances, stabilizes, harmonizes, and heals from a cellular level. It is useful in creating harmony between the chakras, regenerating cells, establishing yin/yang polarity, drawing love, healing heartache and love loss, encouraging creativity, and providing protection. Use it for the metabolism, the endocrine system, the heart, the lungs, and all emotional problems.

Turquoise

A master healer, turquoise protects, calms, balances, grounds, draws prosperity and good luck, aligns the chakras, enhances creativity, balances the female/male energies, bestows mental clarity, absorbs negativity, and increases psychic abilities. It is also helpful for fear, grief, guilt, and lack of peace. Use it for the heart, the chest, the neck, the lungs, the respiratory system, the eyes, cataracts, regenerating tissue, emotional and mental problems, circulation, headaches, and skin disorders. This stone should never be cleaned with salt or salt water.

Source List

I consider these mail order businesses to be reputable and reliable sources for purchasing stones, incenses, and other magical items.

Azure Green
P.O. Box 48
Middlefield, MA 01243-0048
Web site: www.Azuregreen.com
E-mail: AbyssDist@aol.com
Stones, statues, jewelry, books, incenses, and many other items. Free catalog.

Crescent Moongoddess
P.O. Box 153
Massapequa Park, NY 11762
Web site: www.crescentmoongoddess.com
E-mail: cresmoon@crescentmoongoddess.com
Wonderful supply of beautiful, handmade wands, incenses, books, and many other items. Write or e-mail for catalog.

The Mystic Trader
1334 Pacific Avenue
Forest Grove, OR 97116
Web site: www.mystictrader.com
Wide range of unusual items, plus statues, jewelry, and stones. Write for catalog.

Bibliography

_____. *The Audubon Society Field Guide to North American Rocks & Minerals.* NY: Alfred A. Knopf, 1978.

Anderson, Frank J. *Riches of the Earth: Ornamental, Precious & Semiprecious Stones.* NY: Windward, 1981.

Arem, Joel E. *Color Encyclopedia of Gemstones.* NY: Van Nostrand Reinhold, 1977.

Axon, Gordon V. *The Wonderful World of Gems.* NY: Criterion Books, 1967.

Baer, Randall N. & Vicki V. *Windows of Light: Quartz Crystals & Self-Transformation.* NY: Harper & Row, 1984.

_____. *The Crystal Connection: A Guidebook for Personal & Planetary Ascension.* NY: Harper & Row, 1987.

Bancroft, Peter. *The World's Finest Minerals & Crystals.* NY: Viking, 1973.

Bauer, Jaroslav. *A Field Guide in Color to Minerals, Rocks & Precious Stones.* UK: Octopus Books, 1974.

Bell, Pat & Wright, David. *Rocks & Minerals.* NY: Macmillan, 1985.

Bhattacharya, A. K. *Gem Therapy.* Calcutta, India: Firma KLM Private Ltd., 1992.

Boegel, Hellmuth. *The Studio Handbook of Minerals.* NY: Viking, 1972.

Bonewitz, Ra. *Cosmic Crystals.* San Bernardino, CA: The Borgo Press, 1987.

Bowman, Catherine. *Crystal Awareness.* St. Paul, MN: Llewellyn Publications, 1996.

Bryant, Page. *The Magic of Minerals.* Santa Fe, NM: Sun Publishing, 1987.

Budge, E. A. Wallis. *Amulets & Superstitions.* NY: Dover Publications, 1978. Originally published 1930.

Burbutis, Phillip W. *Quartz Crystals for Healing & Meditation.* Tucson, AZ: Universarium Foundation, 1983.

Camp, John. *Magic, Myth & Medicine.* NY: Taplinger, 1974.

Cayce, Edgar. *Gems & Stones.* Virginia Beach, VA: A.R.E. Press, 1960.

Chocron, Daya Sarai. *Healing With Crystals & Gemstones.* York Beach, MA: Samuel Weiser, 1986.

Cipriani, Nicola. *The Encyclopedia of Rocks & Minerals.* NY: Barnes & Noble, 1996.

Clark, Andrew. *Rocks & Minerals.* NY: Exeter Books, 1984.

Conway, D. J. *Celtic Magic.* St. Paul, MN: Llewellyn, 1990.

_____. *Crystal Enchantments.* Watsonville, CA: Crossing Press, 1999.

Court, Arthur & Campbell, Ian. *Minerals: Nature's Fabulous Jewels.* NY: Harry N. Abrams, 1974.

Cunningham, Scott. *Cunningham's Encyclopedia of Crystal, Gem & Metal Magic.* St. Paul, MN: Llewellyn Publications, 1990

_____ & Harrington, David. *Spell Crafts: Creating Magical Objects.* St. Paul, MN: Llewellyn, 1993.

Dake, H. C., Fleener, Frank L., & Wilson, Ben Hur. *Quartz Family Minerals.* NY: McGraw-Hill, 1938.

David, Judithann H. & Van Hulle, J. P. *Michael's Gemstone Dictionary.* Orinda, CA: Affinity Press, 1990.

Deeson, A. F. L. *The Collector's Encyclopedia of Rocks & Minerals.* NY: Clarkson N. Potter, 1973.

Desautels, Paul E. *The Mineral Kingdom.* NY: Grosset & Dunlap, 1968.

_____. *Rocks & Minerals.* NY: Grosset & Dunlap, 1974.

_____. *The Gem Kingdom.* NY: Random House, no date.

Dolfyn. *Crystal Wisdom: A Beginner's Guide, Vol. I & II.* Novato, CA: Earthspirit, 1987.

Fernie, P. J., M.D. *The Occult & Curative Powers of Precious Stones.* San Francisco, CA: Harper & Row, 1973.

Fisher, P. J. *The Science of Gems.* NY: Scribner's, 1966.

Fuller, Sue. *Pocket's Rocks & Minerals.* UK: Dorling Kindersley, 1995.

Gait, Robert I. *Exploring Minerals & Crystals.* Toronto: McGraw-Hill Ryerson, 1972.

Galde, Phyllis. *Crystal Healing.* St. Paul, MN: Llewellyn Publications, 1991.

Gardner, Joy. *Color & Crystals.* Freedom, CA: The Crossing Press, 1988.

Gifford, Edward S., Jr. *The Evil Eye.* NY: Macmillan, 1958.

Gonzalez-Wippler, Migene. *The Complete Book of Amulets & Talismans*. St. Paul, MN: Llewellyn Publications, 1991.

Hall, Callie. *Gem Stones*. NY: DK Publishing, 1994.

Harding, M. Esther. *Woman's Mysteries: Ancient & Modern*. Boston, MA: Shambhala, 1990.

Harford, Virginia & Milewski, John V. *The Crystal Sourcebook: From Science to Metaphysics*. Santa Fe, NM: Mystic Crystal Publications, 1987.

Harold, Edmund. *Focus on Crystals*. NY: Ballantine Books, 1987.

Hay, John. *Kernels of Energy, Bones of Earth: The Rock in Chinese Art*. NY: China House Gallery, 1985.

Hodges, Doris M. *Healing Stones*. Perry, IA: Pyramid Publishers of Iowa, 1985.

Iorusso, Julia & Glick, Joel. *Healing Stoned: The Therapeutic Use of Gems & Minerals*. Albuquerque, NM: Brotherhood of Life, 1985.

Isaacs, Thelma. *Gemstone & Crystal Energies*. Black Mountain, NC: Lorien House, 1989.

Jobes, Gertrude. *Dictionary of Mythology, Folklore & Symbols*. 3 vols. NY: Scarecrow Press, 1962.

Jones, Wendy & Barry. *The Magick of Crystals*. Australia: Harper Collins, 1996.

Keyte, Geoffrey. *The Healing Crystal*. UK: Blandford, 1989.

Kozminsky, Isidore. *The Magic & Science of Jewels & Stones*. Vol. 1 & 2. San Rafael, CA: Cassandra Press, 1988.

Kunz, George Frederick. *The Curious Lore of Precious Stones*. NY: Dover Publications, 1971. Originally printed 1913.

_____. *The Mystical Lore of Precious Stones*. N. Hollywood, CA: Newcastle Publishing, 1986.

_____. *Rings For the Finger*. NY: Dover Publications, 1973. Originally published 1917.

Lorusso, Julia & Glick, Joel. *Healing Stoned: The Therapeutic Use of Gems & Minerals*. Albuquerque, NM: Brotherhood of Life, 1985.

Lucas, Randolph, ed. *The Illustrated Encyclopedia of Minerals & Rocks*. UK: Octopus Books, 1977.

Lyman, Kennie, ed. *Simon & Schuster's Guide to Gems & Precious Stones*. NY: Simon & Schuster, 1986.

Mendenbach, Olaf & Wilk, Harry. *The Magic of Minerals.* Berlin: Springer-Verlag, 1985.

Metz, Rudolph. *Precious Stones & Other Crystals.* NY: Viking, 1965.

Nassau, Kurt. *Gems Made by Man.* Radnor, PA: Chilton, 1980.

_____. *Gemstone Enhancement.* UK: Butterworth's, 1984.

O'Donoghue, Michael. *A Guide to Man-Made Gemstones.* NY: Van Nostrand Reinhold, 1983.

_____. *Quartz.* UK: Butterworth's, 1987.

_____. ed. *The Encyclopedia of Minerals & Gemstones.* NY: Crescent Books, 1983.

Parkinson, Cornelia M. *Gem Magic.* NY: Fawcett Columbine, 1988.

Raphaell, Katrina. *Crystal Enlightenment: The Transforming Properties of Crystals & Healing Stones.* Santa Fe, NM: Aurora Press, 1985.

Ravenwolf, Silver. *To Ride a Silver Broomstick.* St. Paul, MN: Llewellyn, 1993.

Rea, John D. *Patterns of the Whole: Vol. 1, Healing & Quartz Crystals.* Boulder, CO: Two Trees Publishing, 1986.

Rice, Patty C. *Amber: The Golden Gem of the Ages.* NY: Van Nostrand Reinhold, 1980.

Richardson, Wally & Huett, Lenora. *Spiritual Value of Gem Stones.* Marina del Rey, CA: DeVorss & Co., 1980.

Rouse, John D. *Garnet.* UK: Butterworth's, 1986.

Rutland, E. H. *An Introduction to the World's Gemstones.* NY: Doubleday, 1974.

Sanborn, William B. *Oddities of the Mineral World.* NY: Van Nostrand Reinhold, 1976.

Schumann, Walter. *Gemstones of the World.* NY: Sterling, 1977.

Seligmann, Kurt. *Magic, Supernaturalism & Religion.* NY: Pantheon, 1948.

Silbey, Uma. *The Complete Crystal Guidebook.* NY: Bantam Books, 1987.

Sinkankas, John. *Gemstones of North America.* Princeton, NJ: D. Van Nostrand, 1959.

Smith, G. F. Herbert. *Gemstones.* NY: Pitman, 1958.

Smith, Michael G. *Crystal Power.* St. Paul, MN: Llewellyn Publications, 1985.

_____. *Crystal Spirit.* St. Paul, MN: Llewellyn, 1990.

_____. *Crystal Warrior: Shamanic Transformation & Projection of Universal Energy.* St. Paul, MN: Llewellyn Publications, 1993.

Sofianides, Anna S., Harlow, George E., et al. *Gems, Crystals & Minerals.* NY: Simon & Schuster, 1990.

Spencer, L. J. *A Key to Precious Stones.* NY: Emerson Books, 1959.

Stafford, Penny. *Healing Stones.* Minneapolis, MN: self-published, no date.

Stein, Diane. *The Women's Book of Healing.* St. Paul, MN: Llewellyn, 1993.

_____. *The Women's Spirituality Book.* St. Paul, MN: Llewellyn, 1987.

Stern, Max & Company. *Gems: Facts, Fantasies, Superstitions, Legends.* NY: Max Stern & Co., 1946.

Sullivan, Kevin. *The Crystal Handbook.* NY: Signet, 1987.

Thomas, William & Pavitt, Kate. *The Book of Talismans, Amulets & Zodiacal Gems.* N. Hollywood, CA: Wilshire Book Co., 1970.

Thomson, Horace L. *Legends of Gems.* Los Angeles, CA: Graphic Press, 1937.

Troyer, Patricia. *Crystal Personalities: A Quick Reference to Special Forms of Crystal.* Peoria, AZ: Stone People Publishing Co., 1995.

Trussell, Daniel. *Mineral Attunements For Healing & Development.* Atlanta, GA: Browning Press, 1987.

Uyldert, Mellie. *The Magic of Precious Stones.* UK: Turnstone Press, 1981.

Wade, Frank B. *A Text-Book of Precious Stones.* NY: Putnam's, 1918.

Walker, Barbara G. *The Book of Sacred Stones.* San Francisco, CA: HarperCollins, 1989.

_____. *The Woman's Dictionary of Symbols & Sacred Objects.* San Francisco, CA: Harper & Row, 1988.

Webster, Robert. *Gems: Their Sources, Descriptions & Identification.* UK: Butterworth's, 1983.

Weinstein, Michael. *The World of Jewel Stones.* NY: Sheridan House, 1958.

Whitlock, Herbert P. *The Story of the Gems.* NY: Emerson Books, 1963.

Wodiska, Julius. *A Book of Precious Stones.* NY: Putnam's, 1909.

Woolley, Alan, ed. *The Illustrated Encyclopedia of the Mineral Kingdom.* NY: Larousse, 1978.

Zim, Herbert S. & Shaffer, Paul R. *Rocks & Minerals: A Guide to Familiar Minerals, Gems, Ores & Rocks.* NY: Golden Press, 1957.

Index

BOOKS BY THE CROSSING PRESS

Crystal Enchantments: A Complete Guide to Stones and Their Magical Properties

By D. J. Conway

D. J. Conway's book will help guide you in your choice of stones from Adularia to Zircon, by listing their physical properties and magical uses. It will also appeal to folks who are not into magic, but simply love stones and want to know more about them.

$18.95 • Paper • ISBN 1-58091-010-6

Healing with Flower and Gemstone Essences

By Diane Stein

Instructions for choosing and using flowers and gems are combined with descriptions of their effect on emotional balance. Includes instructions for making flower essences and for matching essences to hara line chakras for maximum benefit.

$14.95 • Paper • ISBN 0-89594-856-7

Healing with Gemstones and Crystals

By Diane Stein

More than 200 gemstones and their healing properties are listed. Details on how to choose and use the Earth's precious gems are supplemented by explanations of the significance of this type of healing.

$14.95 • Paper • ISBN 0-89594-831-1

To receive a current catalog from The Crossing Press please call toll-free, 800-777-1048.
Visit our Web site: **www.crossingpress.com**